AMERICAN INDEPENDENCE
AND THE FRENCH REVOLUTION
(1760-1801)

AMERICAN INDEPENDENCE
AND THE FRENCH REVOLUTION (1760-1801)

SAMUEL EDWARD WINBOLT,
KENNETH BELL

ISBN: 978-93-89679-56-4

Published: 1912

LECTOR HOUSE LLP
E-MAIL: lectorpublishing@gmail.com

BELL'S ENGLISH HISTORY SOURCE BOOKS

AMERICAN INDEPENDENCE
AND
THE FRENCH REVOLUTION
(1760-1801)

COMPILED BY

S. E. WINBOLT, M.A.

(CHRIST'S HOSPITAL)

EDITED BY
S. E. WINBOLT, M.A., AND KENNETH BELL, M.A.

1912

CONTENTS

INTRODUCTION

This series of English History Source Books is intended for use with any ordinary textbook of English History. Experience has conclusively shown that such apparatus is a valuable—nay, an indispensable—adjunct to the history lesson. It is capable of two main uses: either by way of lively illustration at the close of a lesson, or by way of inference-drawing, before the textbook is read, at the beginning of the lesson. The kind of problems and exercises that may be based on the documents are legion, and are admirably illustrated in a *History of England for Schools*, Part I., by Keatinge and Frazer, pp. 377-381. However, we have no wish to prescribe for the teacher the manner in which he shall exercise his craft, but simply to provide him and his pupils with materials hitherto not readily accessible for school purposes. The very moderate price of the books in this series should bring them within the reach of every secondary school. Source books enable the pupil to take a more active part than hitherto in the history lesson. Here is the apparatus, the raw material: its use we leave to teacher and taught.

Our belief is that the books may profitably be used by all grades of historical students between the standards of fourth-form boys in secondary schools and undergraduates at Universities. What differentiates students at one extreme from those at the other is not so much the kind of subject-matter dealt with, as the amount they can read into or extract from it.

In regard to choice of subject-matter, while trying to satisfy the natural demand for certain "stock" documents of vital importance, we hope to introduce much fresh and novel matter. It is our intention that the majority of the extracts should be lively in style—that is, personal, or descriptive, or rhetorical, or even strongly partisan—and should not so much profess to give the truth as supply data for inference. We aim at the greatest possible variety, and lay under contribution letters, biographies, ballads and poems, diaries, debates, and newspaper accounts. Economics, London, municipal, and social life generally, and local history, are represented in these pages.

The order of the extracts is strictly chronological, each being numbered, titled, and dated, and its authority given. The text is modernised, where necessary, to the extent of leaving no difficulties in reading.

We shall be most grateful to teachers and students who may send us suggestions for improvement.

S. E. WINBOLT.
KENNETH BELL.

NOTE TO THIS VOLUME
(1760-1801)

The difficulty which an editor of period 1760-1801 has to face is the wealth of contemporary sources available. I have drawn largely, as will be seen, on the series of Home Office Papers in the Calendar of State Papers, the series of the Acts of the Privy Council, the *Gentleman's Magazine*, and *Annual Register*. I trust that the foreign relations of England are proportionately represented, though want of space has been against the inclusion of much that naturally suggests itself. In spite of defects, my hope is that teachers and pupils in public schools and universities will find these pages useful.

S. E. W.

CHRIST'S HOSPITAL,
April, 1912.

AMERICAN INDEPENDENCE AND THE FRENCH REVOLUTION (1760-1801)

BRITISH VICTORIES—"A YOUNG MR. BURKE" (1761).

Source.—*Letters of Horace Walpole.* Edited by P. Cunningham
London: Bentley. Vol. iii., pp. 419-421. 1891.

Horace Walpole

To George Montagu, Esq., Strawberry Hill, July 22, 1761.

For my part, I believe Mademoiselle Scuderi drew the plan of this year. It is all royal marriages, coronations and victories; they come tumbling so over one another from distant parts of the globe, that it looks just like the handy-work of a lady romance writer, whom it costs nothing but a little false geography to make the great Mogul in love with a princess of — —, and defeat two marshals of France as he rides post on an elephant to his nuptials. I don't know where I am. I had scarce found Mecklenburgh Strelitz with a magnifying glass, before I am whisked to Pondicherri—well, I take it, and raze it. I begin to grow acquainted with Colonel Coote, and to figure him packing up chests of diamonds, and sending them to his wife against the King's wedding—thunder go the Tower guns, and behold Broglio and Soubise are totally defeated; if the mob have not much stronger heads and quicker conceptions than I have, they will conclude my lord Granby is become nabob. How the deuce in two days can one digest all this? Why is not Pondicherri in Westphalia? I don't know how the Romans did, but I cannot support two victories every week. Well, but you will want to know the particulars. Broglio and Soubise, united, attacked our army on the fifteenth, but were repulsed; the next day, the prince Mahomet Alli Cawn—no, no, I mean prince Ferdinand, returned the attack, and the French threw down their arms, and fled, run over my lord Harcourt, who was going to fetch the new queen; in short, I don't know how it was, but Mr. Conway is safe, and I am as happy as Mr. Pitt himself. We have only lost a lieutenant-colonel Keith; colonel Marlay and Harry Townshend are wounded.... I dined with your secretary yesterday; there were Garrick and a young Mr. Burke, who wrote a book in the style of lord Bolingbroke, that was much admired. He is a sensible man, but has not worn off his authorism yet, and thinks there is nothing so charming as writers, and to be one. He will know better one of these days. I like Hamilton's little Marly; we walked in the great allée, and drank tea in the arbour of treillage; they talked of Shakspeare and Booth, of Swift and my lord Bath, and I was thinking of Madame Sévigné. Good night! I have a dozen other letters to write; I must tell my friends how happy I am—not as an Englishman, but as a cousin.

Yours ever.

HONOURS FOR MR. PITT (1761).

Source.—*Correspondence of William Pitt, Earl of Chatham.* Vol. ii., pp. 146 *et seq.* London, 1838-1840.

Correspondence of Chatham

The Earl of Bute to Mr. Pitt, October 6, 1761.

Sir,

I take up the pen with more than ordinary desire to succeed in the business I am, by the King's command, to write to you upon. I earnestly wished to have carried to his Majesty some little opening of your mind; something that might have pointed towards that mark of his royal favour he seems impatient to bestow upon you.[1]

As that was not in my power, the King has desired me to mention two ideas; wishing to have the one most agreeable to you carried into immediate execution: but, if neither should be suitable to your inclinations, it is hoped that you will not be averse to give his Majesty a little insight into your own thoughts upon this subject. The government of the province of Canada, with a salary of five thousand pounds, seemed to strike the King most; and that for two reasons: the first, as you would preside over a province acquired by your own ability and firmness; secondly, as it would convey to all the world his Majesty's intentions of never parting with that great and important conquest. The objection of its not being tenable with a seat in parliament is foreseen; but a short bill might remedy that in this new case;

---

[1] Mr. Burke, who wrote the historical portion of the *Annual Register* for the year 1761, says, that "when Mr. Pitt resigned the seals, the great person to whom they were re-delivered received them with ease and firmness, without requesting that he should resume his office. His Majesty expressed his concern for the loss of so able a servant; and to show the favourable sense he entertained of his services, he made him a most gracious and unlimited offer of any rewards in the power of the Crown to bestow. His Majesty at the same time expressed himself not only satisfied with the opinion of the majority of his council, but declared he would have found himself under the greatest difficulty how to have acted, had that council concurred as fully in supporting the measure proposed by Mr. Pitt as they had done in rejecting it. Mr. Pitt was sensibly touched with the grandeur and condescension of the proceeding. 'I confess, sir, I had but too much reason to expect your Majesty's displeasure: I did not come prepared for this exceeding goodness: pardon me, Sir,—it overpowers, it oppresses me.' He burst into tears. We are far from an attempt to add any colouring to so exquisitely affecting a picture; we are, indeed, far from being able to do justice to perhaps one of the most pathetic and elevated scenes which could possibly be displayed,—the parting of such a prince, and such a minister."

in the preamble of which the King's reasons for this appointment would be set forth. If, however, this should not strike you in the same light it does his Majesty, the next thing I am ordered to mention is the chancellor of the duchy, with the salary annexed to it as before mentioned.

You will please, Sir, to consider these as proofs of the King's earnest desire to show this country the high opinion he has of your merit. If they do not entirely please, impute it to the want of information I before hinted at; and do me the justice to believe, that I never shall execute any commission with more pleasure than I have done this.

I am, Sir, with the highest regard,
Your most obedient humble servant,
BUTE.[2]

Mr. Pitt to the Earl of Bute, October 7, 1761.

[From a rough draught in Mr. Pitt's handwriting.]

MY LORD,

Overwhelmed with the extent of his Majesty's gracious goodness towards me, I desire the favour of your Lordship to lay me at the royal feet, with the humble tribute of the most unfeigned and respectful gratitude. Penetrated with the bounteous favour of a most benign sovereign and master, I am confounded with his condescension in deigning to bestow one thought about any inclination of his servant, with regard to the modes of extending to me marks of his royal beneficence.

Any public mark of his Majesty's approbation, flowing from such a spontaneous source of clemency, will be my comfort and my glory; and I cannot but be highly sensible of all those circumstances, so peculiarly honourable, which, attending the first of the two ideas suggested to me by his Majesty's direction, have been mentioned. Commanded, however, as I am by the King, in a manner so infinitely gracious, not to suppress my thoughts on a subject of this extreme delicacy, I trust it will be judged obedience, not presumption, if I express the doubts I

---

[2] On the evening of this day Bubb Doddington (now Lord Melcombe) wrote thus to Lord Bute: "I sincerely wish your lordship joy of being delivered of a most impracticable colleague, his Majesty of a most imperious servant, and the country of a most dangerous minister. I am told that the people are sullen about it. Be that as it may, I think it my duty to my gracious Sovereign and my generous friend to say, that, if I can be of any service to either in anything that is most dangerous and difficult, I am most ready to undertake it." In his answer of the following day, Lord Bute says: "Whatever private motives of uneasiness I might have in the late administration, I am far from thinking the dissolution of it favourable, in the present minute, to the King's affairs. I shall not fail to acquaint the King with the very frank and generous declaration you made. Indeed, my good lord, my situation, at all times perilous, is become much more so; for I am no stranger to the language held in this great city: 'Our darling's resignation is owing to Lord Bute, and he must answer for all the consequences;'—which is, in other words, for the miscarriages of another system, that Pitt himself would not have prevented. All this keeps up my attention, and strengthens my mind, without alarming it; not only whispers caution, but steadiness and resolution; wherein my noble friend's assistance will prove a real comfort to me."

have as to the propriety of my going into either of the offices mentioned, or indeed, considering that which I have resigned, going again into any whatever.

Thus much in general I have presumed, not without pain and fear, to submit to his Majesty's consideration; too proud to receive any mark of the King's countenance and favour, but above all doubly happy could I see those dearer to me than myself comprehended in that monument of royal approbation and goodness, with which his Majesty shall condescend to distinguish me.

I cannot conclude this letter, already much too long, without expressing my warm thanks to your Lordship for the most obliging manner in which you have conveyed to me his Majesty's gracious intentions, and assuring your Lordship, that I shall always set a high value on the favourable sentiments which you are pleased to express on my subject. I have the honour to be, with great truth and respect,

Yours, &c.
W. Pitt.

The Earl of Bute to Mr. Pitt, October 8, 1761.

Sir,

I laid the contents of your letter before his Majesty; who was graciously pleased to admit of the reasons you gave for not accepting office, and to approve of the respectful openings some part of the letter afforded.

Having received the King's commands to consider of the most becoming method of carrying his intentions into execution, I have lost no time in my researches. The English civil list would by no means answer; the Irish had objections: one only thing remained, that could possibly serve the King's generous purpose. This his Majesty approves of, and has directed me accordingly to acquaint you, that as you declined accepting any office, his Majesty will confer the dignity of peerage on Lady Hester Pitt, to descend through her ladyship to your sons, with a grant of three thousand pounds per annum, on the plantation duties, to yourself and any two other lives you shall name. These unusual marks of the royal approbation cannot fail to be agreeable to a mind like yours. Permit me to assure you, that the communicating of them gives me the greatest pleasure.

I am, Sir, with unfeigned regard,
Your most obedient humble servant,
Bute.

Mr. Pitt to the Earl of Bute, October 8, 1761.

[From a draught in Mr. Pitt's handwriting.]

I have not words to express the sentiments of veneration and gratitude with which I receive the unbounded effects of beneficence and grace, which the most benign of sovereigns has condescended to bestow on me, and on those most dear to me.

Your Lordship will not wonder if the sensations which possess my whole breast refuse me the power of describing their extent, and leave me only to beg your Lordship will be so good as to lay me and Lady Hester at the King's feet, and to offer for us to his Majesty the genuine tribute of the truly feeling heart; which I will dare to hope, the same royal benevolence which showers on the unmeritorious such unlimited benefits may deign to accept with equal condescension and goodness.

I am, &c.
W. Pitt.

THE STATE OF THE PRISONS.

Source.—Goldsmith's *Vicar of Wakefield* (Chap. XXVII.).

Goldsmith

The next morning I communicated to my wife and children the scheme I had planned of reforming the prisoners, which they received with universal disapprobation, alleging the impossibility and impropriety of it; adding that my endeavours would no way contribute to their amendment, but might probably disgrace my calling.

"Excuse me," returned I, "these people, however fallen, are still men; and that is a very good title to my affections. Good counsel rejected returns to enrich the giver's bosom; and though the instruction I communicate may not mend them, yet it will assuredly mend myself. If these wretches, my children, were princes, there would be thousands ready to offer their ministry; but in my opinion the heart that is buried in a dungeon is as precious as that seated upon a throne. Yes, my treasures, if I can mend them I will; perhaps they will not all despise me; perhaps I may catch up even one from the gulf, and there will be great gain; for is there upon earth a gem so precious as the human soul?"

Thus saying, I left them and descended to the common prison, where I found the prisoners very merry, expecting my arrival; and each prepared with some gaol-trick to play upon the doctor. Thus, as I was going to begin, one turned my wig awry; as if by accident, and then asked my pardon. A second, who stood at some distance, had a knack of spitting through his teeth, which fell in showers upon my book. A third would cry, "Amen!" in such an affected tone as gave the rest great delight. A fourth had slily picked my pocket of my spectacles. But there was one whose trick gave more universal pleasure than all the rest; for observing the manner in which I had disposed my books on the table before me, he very dexterously displaced one of them, and put an obscene jest-book of his own in the place. However, I took no notice of all that this mischievous group of little beings could do, but went on, perfectly sensible that what was ridiculous in my attempt would excite mirth only the first or second time, while what was serious would be permanent. My design succeeded, and in less than six days some were penitent, and all attentive.

It was now that I applauded my perseverance and address, at thus giving sensibility to wretches divested of every moral feeling, and now began to think of doing them temporal service also, by rendering their situation somewhat more comfortable. Their time had hitherto been divided between famine and excess, tumultuous riot and bitter repining. Their only employment was quarrelling among each other, playing at cribbage, and cutting tobacco-stoppers. From this last mode of idle industry I took the hint of setting such as chose to work at cutting pegs for tobacconists and shoemakers, the proper wood being bought by a general subscription, and, when manufactured, sold by my appointment; so that each earned something every day—a trifle, indeed, but sufficient to maintain him.

I did not stop here, but instituted fines for the punishment of immorality, and rewards for peculiar industry. Thus in less than a fortnight I had formed them into something social and humane, and had the pleasure of regarding myself as a legislator, who had brought men from their native ferocity into friendship and obedience.

And it were highly to be wished that legislative power would thus direct the law rather to reformation than to severity; that it would seem convinced that the work of eradicating crimes is not by making punishments familiar, but formidable. Then, instead of our present prisons, which find or make men guilty, which enclose wretches for the commission of one crime, and return them, if returned alive, fitted for the perpetration of thousands, we should see, as in other parts of Europe, places of penitence and solitude, where the accused might be attended by such as could give them repentance if guilty, or new motives to virtue if innocent. And this, but not the increasing punishments, is the way to mend a State: nor can I avoid even questioning the validity of that right which social combinations have assumed of capitally punishing offences of a slight nature. In cases of murder, their right is obvious, as it is the duty of us all, from the law of self-defence, to cut off that man who has shown a disregard for the life of another. Against such all nature rises in arms, but it is not so against him who steals my property. Natural law gives me no right to take away his life, as by that the horse he steals is as much his property as mine. If, then, I have any right, it must be from a compact made between us, that he who deprives the other of his horse shall die. But this is a false compact; because no man has a right to barter his life, any more than to take it away, as it is not his own. And, besides, the compact is inadequate, and would be set aside even in a court of modern equity, as there is a great penalty for a very trifling inconvenience, since it is far better that two men should live than that one man should ride. But a compact that is false between two men is equally so between a hundred and a hundred thousand; for as ten millions of circles can never make a square, so the united voice of myriads cannot lend the smallest foundation to falsehood. It is thus that reason speaks, and untutored nature says the same thing. Savages that are directed by natural law alone are very tender of the lives of each other; they seldom shed blood but to retaliate former cruelty.

Our Saxon ancestors, fierce as they were in war, had but few executions in times of peace; and in all commencing governments, that have the print of nature still strong upon them, scarcely any crime is held capital.

It is among the citizens of a refined community that penal laws, which are in the hands of the rich, are laid upon the poor. Government, while it grows older, seems to acquire the moroseness of age; and as if our property were become dearer in proportion as it increased—as if the more enormous our wealth, the more extensive our fears—all our possessions are paled up with new edicts every day, and hung round with gibbets to scare every invader.

I cannot tell whether it is from the number of our penal laws, or the licentiousness of our people, that this country should show more convicts in a year than half the dominions of Europe united. Perhaps it is owing to both; for they mutually produce each other. When by indiscriminate penal laws a nation beholds the same punishment affixed to dissimilar degrees of guilt, from perceiving no distinction in the penalty, the people are led to lose all sense of distinction in the crime; and this distinction is the bulwark of all morality: thus the multitude of laws produce new vices, and new vices call for fresh restraints.

It were to be wished, then, that power, instead of contriving new laws to punish vice, instead of drawing hard the cords of society till a convulsion come to burst them, instead of cutting away wretches as useless before we have tried their utility, instead of converting correction into vengeance; it were to be wished that we tried the restrictive arts of government, and made law the protector, but not the tyrant, of the people. We should then find that creatures, whose souls are held as dross, only wanted the hand of a refiner; we should then find that wretches, now stuck up for long tortures, lest luxury should feel a momentary pang, might, if properly treated, serve to sinew the State in times of danger; that as their faces are like ours, their hearts are so too; that few minds are so base as that perseverance cannot amend; that a man may see his last crime without dying for it; and that very little blood will serve to cement our security.

TOWNSHEND'S CONTUMACY (1767).

Source. — *Correspondence of William Pitt, Earl of Chatham.* Vol. iii.,
pp. 233 *et seq.* London, 1838-1840.

Correspondence of Chatham: Shelburne and Burke

Mr. Townshend then mentioned the extraordinaries of America, and the necessity of voting a particular sum; which he said he neither could nor would move, unless the cabinet previously took the whole state of America into consideration, and enabled him to declare to the House the opinion of administration as to the forts, the Indian trade, the disposition of the troops, in short the whole arrangements, considered with a view to a general reduction of expense, and a duty which he undertook should be laid to defray what remained: that he had promised this to the House, and upon the authority of what passed in the cabinet; and if he could not make it good, he should be obliged to consider the best means, by what he should say or by his conduct, to make it appear that it was not his fault, and against his opinion.[3]

[3] It is impossible to read this letter without being forcibly reminded of the following splendid passages in Mr. Burke's celebrated speech, in 1774, on American taxation:

"If ever Lord Chatham fell into a fit of the gout, or if any other cause withdrew him from public cares, principles directly the contrary of his own were sure to predominate. When his face was hid but for a moment, his whole system was on a wide sea, without chart or compass. The gentlemen, his particular friends, who, with the names of various departments of ministry, were admitted to seem as if they acted a part under him, with a modesty that becomes all men, and with a confidence in him, which was justified even in its extravagance by his superior abilities, had never, in any instance, presumed upon any opinion of their own. Deprived of his guiding influence, they were whirled about, the sport of every gust, and easily driven into any port; and as those who joined with them in manning the vessel were the most directly opposite to his opinions, measures, and character, and far the most artful and most powerful of the set, they easily prevailed so as to seize upon the vacant, unoccupied, and derelict minds of his friends; and instantly they turned the vessel wholly out of the course of his policy. As if it were to insult as well as to betray him, even long before the close of the first session of his administration, when everything was publicly transacted, and with great parade, in his name, they made an act declaring it highly just and expedient to raise a revenue in America. For even then, Sir, even before this splendid orb was entirely set, and while the western horizon was in a blaze with his descending glory, on the opposite quarter of the heavens arose another luminary, and, for his hour, became lord of the ascendant. You understand, to be sure, that I speak of Charles Townshend, officially the reproducer of this fatal scheme...."

"He had voted, and in the year 1765, had been an advocate for the stamp act. Things, and the disposition of men's minds, were changed. In short, the stamp act began to be no

I acquainted your Lordship of this the last time I had the honour of waiting on you from Lord Barrington; the difficulty greatly arising from several conjectural estimates being laid by him before the House. I was surprised at Mr. Townshend's conduct, which really continues excessive on every occasion, till I afterwards understood in conversation, that he declared he knew of Lord North's refusal, and from himself. The Duke of Grafton told me, and I suppose may tell your Lordship, that he sent to Lord North to ask him. It appears to me quite impossible that Mr. Townshend can mean to go on in the King's service; but of this your Lordship will judge much better than I can, after the Duke of Grafton has given you a farther account.

I have the honour to be, with great respect, Your Lordship's most obliged humble servant, SHELBURNE.

---

favourite in this House. He, therefore, attended at the private meeting, in which the resolutions moved by a right honourable gentleman were settled; resolutions leading to the repeal. The next day, he voted for that repeal; and he would have spoken for it, too, if an illness (not, as was then given out, a political), but, to my knowledge, a very real illness, had not prevented it. The very next session, as the fashion of this world passeth away, the repeal began to be in as bad an odour in this House as the stamp act had been in the session before. To conform to the temper which began to prevail, and to prevail mostly amongst those most in power, he declared, very early in the winter, that a revenue must be had out of America. Instantly he was tied down to his engagements by some who had no objection to such experiments at the cost of persons for whom they had no particular regard. The whole body of courtiers drove him onwards. They always talked as if the King stood in a sort of humiliated state, until something of the kind should be done. Here this extraordinary man, then Chancellor of the Exchequer, found himself in great straits. To please universally was the object of his life; but to tax and to please, no more than to love and to be wise, is not given to men. However, he attempted it. To render a tax palatable to the partisans of American revenue, he made a preamble, stating the necessity of such a revenue. To close with the American distinction, this revenue was *external*, or port duty; but again, to soften it to the other party, it was a duty of *supply*.

"To gratify the *colonists*, it was laid on British manufactures; to satisfy the *merchants of Britain*, the duty was trivial, and (except that on tea, which touched only the devoted East India Company) on none of the grand objects of commerce. To counterwork the American contraband, the duty on tea was reduced from a shilling to threepence. But to secure the favour of those who would tax America, the scene of collection was changed, and, with the rest, it was levied in the colonies. What need I say more? This fine-spun scheme had the usual fate of all exquisite policy. But the original plan of the duties, and the mode of executing that plan, both arose singly and solely from a love of our applause. He was truly the child of the House. He never thought, did, or said anything, but with a view to you. He every day adapted himself to your disposition; and adjusted himself before it as at a looking-glass. Hence arose this unfortunate act."

WILKES RIOTS (1768).

Source.—*Calendar of Home Office Papers, 1766-1769.* Pp. 322, 323.
London, 1879.

Home Office Papers

Robert Wood to Sir J. Fielding.

5 and 6 April.—Lord Weymouth has been informed that Mr. Stuart, the wine merchant, upon application to you for assistance against the mob on the night of the illumination, had not met with that support which he had reason to expect from the civil magistrate. Though this account does not agree with what his Lordship had conceived of your vigilance and activity, yet he has ordered me to acquaint you with it, and to add that though, on the one hand, he relies much on your zeal, and is ready to do justice to your diligence at the time of the late riotous proceedings, yet, on the other, he thinks it his indispensable duty to take notice of any remissness in a magistrate upon whom so much of the public order and tranquillity depends; and if Mr. Stuart's account of this matter be founded, his Lordship desires that I will let you know it will very much change that favourable opinion which he wishes to preserve of you. His Lordship thinks it would be unfair towards you as well as to the public to keep this matter from you, though Mr. Stuart has not given it in as matter of formal complaint, but merely for the Secretary of State's information. Lord Weymouth is willing to suppose there must be some mistake in what he has heard.

P.S.—As Lord Weymouth had taken every precaution that could be imagined in order to support magistracy and give weight to your proceedings, he is disappointed to find that there should be any complaint; and though he despises clamour, he must pay attention to facts urged by a citizen of character; and I heartily wish you may put it in his power to set you clear of imputation, which is his wish also.

The reply to this letter is dated the 5th.

Sir John Fielding gives a history of the transactions of the night, and says that, to the best of his knowledge, and to the best of his abilities, with unwearied attention, diligence, and application, he has done everything in his power to preserve peace and good order, and to detect offenders and bring them to justice, from the beginning to the conclusion of the late unhappy disturbances. Is sincerely concerned if in any respect Mr. Steward mistook his meaning, and more so that Lord Weymouth should be dissatisfied with his conduct as a magistrate. Unfortunate he has always been; at present particularly so, when his warmest endeavours to discharge a public trust with loyalty to his Sovereign, fidelity to his country, and obedience to his superiors, have been so far ineffectual as not to secure him the confidence of those by whom he would wish to be approved.—Bow Street.

RIOTS IN THE NORTH (1768).

Source.—*Calendar of Home Office Papers, 1766-1769.* Pp. 839, 840.
London, 1879.

Home Office Papers

Duke of Northumberland to H.M.'s Principal Secretaries of State.

12 and 14 April.—Has received within these few days several letters from New-castle, giving an account of a very riotous spirit having broken out among the sailors and other persons in that place and its neighbourhood, who have committed many outrages, a continuance of which is still greatly to be apprehended. His Grace enters into full particulars. The Mayor and other magistrates of Newcastle, and the justices of Northumberland and Durham, have been very vigilant and active on this occasion, but it is their united request, in which his Grace joins, that a regiment might be quartered and continued in Newcastle and the neighbourhood.—Northumberland House, 12 April.

Reply from Lord Weymouth, dated the 14th, enclosing a copy of the letter written in consequence to the Secretary-at-War, directing him to give orders for detaining the troops at Newcastle and the neighbourhood which are now there, and to report whether the present disposition of the troops in that part of the world may not admit of an alteration which may answer the purposes of support to the civil magistrate.

The Same to the Same.

13 and 14 April.—Submitting whether it may not be expedient that certain arms belonging to the Middlesex militia, deposited in the vestry rooms and other places of little security in Westminster and the neighbourhood of London, should be removed to the Tower, in case there should be reason to fear a renewal of the mobs and riotous assemblies.

Lord Weymouth's Reply, dated the 14th.

It is highly improper that arms should at any time be deposited in places of little security, and particularly at present when so riotous a disposition appears among the populace. But as there are objections to depositing those arms now in the Tower, his Grace is to take all possible precautions for the present by giving the necessary orders for particular attention and vigilance upon this occasion; and in case of an attempt by the populace to possess themselves of the arms, is to call out the military, orders having been issued to the Secretary-at-War to support the civil magistrate upon every necessary occasion.

A PETITION TO GEORGE III. FROM THE FREEHOLDERS OF THE COUNTY OF MIDDLESEX (1769).

Source.—*Letters of Junius.* London: G. Bell and Sons. Vol. ii. 1911.

Letters of Junius

To the King's Most Excellent Majesty.

The humble petition of the Freeholders of the County of Middlesex.

MOST GRACIOUS SOVEREIGN,

We, your Majesty's dutiful and loyal subjects, the Freeholders of the County of Middlesex, beg leave, with all affectionate submission and humility, to throw ourselves at your royal feet, and humbly to implore your paternal attention to those grievances of which this county and the whole nation complain, and those fearful apprehensions with which the whole British Empire is most justly alarmed.

With great grief and sorrow we have long beheld the endeavours of certain evil-minded persons, who attempt to infuse into your royal mind notions and opinions of the most dangerous and pernicious tendency, and who promote and counsel such measures as cannot fail to destroy that harmony and confidence which should ever subsist between a just and virtuous prince and a free and loyal people.

For this disaffected purpose they have introduced into every part of the administration of our happy legal constitution a certain unlimited and indefinite discretionary power, to prevent which is the sole aim of all our laws, and was the sole cause of all those disturbances and revolutions which formerly distracted this unhappy country; for our ancestors, by their own fatal experience, well knew that in a state where discretion begins, law, liberty, and safety end. Under the pretence of this discretion, or, as it was formerly, and has been lately, called, Law of state, we have seen

English subjects, and even a member of the British Legislature, arrested by virtue of a general warrant issued by a secretary of state, contrary to the law of the land.

Their houses rifled and plundered, their papers seized, and used as evidence upon trial.

Their bodies committed to close imprisonment.

The Habeas Corpus eluded.

Trial by jury discountenanced, and the first law officer of the crown publicly insinuating that juries are not to be trusted.

Printers punished by the ministry in the supreme court without a trial by their equals, without any trial at all.

The remedy of the law for false imprisonment debarred and defeated.

The plaintiff and his attorney, for their appeal to the law of the land, punished by expenses and imprisonment, and made, by forced engagements, to desist from their legal claim.

A writing determined to be a libel by a court where it was not cognizable in the first instance; contrary to law, because all appeal is thereby cut off, and inferior courts and juries influenced by such predetermination.

A person condemned in the said courts as the author of the supposed libel, unheard, without defence or trial.

Unjust treatment of petitions, by selecting only such parts as might be wrested to criminate the petitioner, and refusing to hear those which might procure him redress.

The thanks of one branch of the Legislature proposed by a minister to be given to an acknowledged offender for his offence, with the declared intention of screening him from the law.

Attachments wrested from their original intent of removing obstructions to the proceedings of law, to punish by sentence of arbitrary fine and imprisonment, without trial or appeal, supposed offences committed out of court.

Perpetual imprisonment of an Englishman without trial, conviction, or sentence, by the same mode of attachment, wherein the same person is at once party, accuser, judge, and jury.

Instead of the ancient and legal civil police, the military introduced at every opportunity, unnecessarily and unlawfully patrolling the streets, to the alarm and terror of the inhabitants.

The lives of many of your Majesty's innocent subjects destroyed by military execution.

Such military execution solemnly adjudged to be legal.

Murder abetted, encouraged, and rewarded.

The civil magistracy rendered contemptible by the appointment of improper and incapable persons.

The civil magistrates tampered with by administration, and neglecting and refusing to discharge their duty.

Mobs and riots hired and raised by the ministry, in order to justify and recommend their own illegal proceedings, and to prejudice your Majesty's mind by false insinuations against the loyalty of your Majesty's subjects.

The freedom of election violated by corrupt and undue influence, by unpunished violence and murder.

The just verdicts of juries and the opinion of the judges overruled by false representations to your Majesty; and the determinations of the law set aside, by new, unprecedented, and dangerous means; thereby leaving the guilty without restraint, and the injured without redress, and the lives of your Majesty's subjects at the mercy of every ruffian protected by administration.

Obsolete and vexatious claims of the crown set on foot for partial and election purposes.

Partial attacks on the liberty of the press, the most daring and pernicious libels against the constitution and against the liberty of the subject being allowed to pass unnoticed, whilst the slightest libel against a minister is punished with the utmost rigour.

Wicked attempts to increase and establish a standing army, by endeavouring to vest in the crown an unlimited power over the militia, which, should they succeed, must, sooner or later, subvert the constitution, by augmenting the power of administration in proportion to their delinquency.

Repeated endeavours to diminish the importance of members of parliament individually, in order to render them more dependent on administration collectively. Even threats having been employed by ministers to suppress the freedom of debate; and the wrath of parliament denounced against measures authorized by the law of the land.

Resolutions of one branch of the legislature set up as the law of the land, being a direct usurpation of the rights of the two other branches, and therefore a manifest infringement of the constitution.

Public money shamefully squandered and unaccounted for, and all inquiry into the cause of arrears in the civil list prevented by the ministry.

Inquiry into a paymaster's public accounts stopped in the exchequer, though the sums accounted for by that paymaster amount to above forty millions sterling.

Public loans perverted to private ministerial purposes.

Prostitution of public honours and rewards to men who can neither plead public virtue nor services.

Irreligion and immorality, so eminently discountenanced by your Majesty's royal example, encouraged by administration, both by example and precept.

The same discretion has been extended by the same evil counsellors to your Majesty's dominions in America, and has produced to our suffering fellow-subjects in that part of the world grievances and apprehensions similar to those which we complain of at home.

MOST GRACIOUS SOVEREIGN,

Such are the grievances and apprehensions which have long discontented and disturbed the greatest and best part of your Majesty's loyal subjects. Unwilling, however, to interrupt your royal repose, though ready to lay down our lives and fortunes for your Majesty's service, and for the constitution as by law established, we have waited patiently, expecting a constitutional remedy by the means of our own representatives, but our legal and free choice having been repeatedly rejected, and the right of election now finally taken from us by the unprecedented seating of a candidate who was never chosen by the county, and who, even to become a candidate, was obliged fraudulently to vacate his seat in parliament, under the pretence of an insignificant place, invited thereto by the prior declaration of a minister, that whoever opposed our choice, though but with four votes, should be declared member for the county. We see ourselves, by this last act, deprived even of the franchises of Englishmen, reduced to the most abject state of slavery, and left without hopes or means of redress but from your Majesty or God.

Deign then, most gracious Sovereign, to listen to the prayer of the most faithful of your Majesty's subjects; and to banish from your royal favour, trust, and confidence, for ever, those evil and pernicious counsellors who have endeavoured to alienate the affection of your Majesty's most sincere and dutiful subjects, and whose suggestions tend to deprive your people of their dearest and most essential rights, and who have traitorously dared to depart from the spirit and letter of those laws which have secured the crown of these realms to the House of Brunswick, in which we make our most earnest prayers to God that it may continue untarnished to the latest posterity.

Signed by 1565 Freeholders.

THE CITY OF LONDON AND THE EARL OF CHATHAM ON PARLIAMENTARY REFORM (1770).

Source.—*Letters of Junius.* London: G. Bell and Sons. 1910. Vol. i.

Letters of Junius

At a Common Council holden on the 14th of May, 1770, it was resolved: "That the grateful thanks of this court be presented to the Right Hon. William Earl of Chatham, for the zeal he has shown in support of those most valuable and sacred privileges, the right of election, and the right of petition; and for his wishes and declaration, that his endeavours shall hereafter be used that parliaments may be restored to their original purity, by shortening their duration, and introducing a more full and equal representation, an act which will render his name more honoured by posterity than the memorable successes of the glorious war he conducted."

To this vote of thanks the Earl of Chatham made the following reply to the committee deputed to present it to his Lordship:

Gentlemen,

It is not easy for me to give expression to all I feel on the extraordinary honour done to my public conduct by the city of London; a body so highly respectable on every account, but above all, for their constant assertion of the birthrights of Englishmen in every great crisis of the constitution.

In our present unhappy situation my duty shall be, on all proper occasions, to add the zealous endeavours of an individual to those legal exertions of constitutional rights, which, to their everlasting honour, the city of London has made in defence of freedom of election and freedom of petition, and for obtaining effectual reparation to the electors of Great Britain.

As to the point among the declarations which I am understood to have made, of my wishes for the public, permit me to say there has been some misapprehension, for with all my deference to the sentiments of the city, I am bound to declare, that I cannot recommend triennial parliaments[4] as a remedy against that canker of the constitution, venality in elections; but I am ready to submit my opinion to better judgment if the wish for that measure shall become prevalent in the king-

[4] On the subject of triennial parliaments, Lord Chatham appears subsequently to have changed his opinion, as will be seen by reference to his speech in the Lords, April 30, 1771, in which he declares himself "a convert to triennial parliaments."

dom. Purity of parliament is the corner-stone in the commonwealth; and as one obvious means towards this necessary end is to strengthen and extend the natural relation between the constituents and the elected, I have, in this view, publicly expressed my earnest wishes for a more full and equal representation by the addition of one knight of the shire in a county, as a further balance to the mercenary boroughs.

I have thrown out this idea with the just diffidence of a private man when he presumes to suggest anything new on a high matter. Animated by your approbation, I shall with better hope continue humbly to submit it to the public wisdom, as an object most deliberately to be weighed, accurately examined, and maturely digested.

Having many times, when in the service of the crown, and when retired from it, experienced, with gratitude, the favour of my fellow-citizens, I am now particularly fortunate, that, with their good liking, I can offer anything towards upholding this wisely-combined frame of mixed government against the decays of time, and the deviations incident to all human institutions; and I shall esteem my life honoured indeed, if the city of London can vouchsafe to think that my endeavours have not been wanting to maintain the national honour, to defend the colonies, and extend the commercial greatness of my country, as well as to preserve from violation the law of the land, and the essential rights of the constitution.

COMMENTS ON PARLIAMENTARY HAPPEN-INGS (DECEMBER, 1770).

Source.—*Letters of Junius* (Letter LXXXI.). London: G. Bell and Sons. 1911. Vol. ii.

Letters of Junius

For the "Public Advertiser," December 14, 1770.

SECOND CHAPTER OF FACTS, OR MATERIALS FOR HISTORY.

1. The Earl of Chatham having asserted, on Tuesday last, in the House of Lords, that Gibraltar was open to an attack from the sea, and that, if the enemy were masters of the bay, the place could not make any long resistance, he was answered in the following words by that great statesman the Earl of Sandwich:—"Supposing the noble Lord's argument to be well founded, and *supposing Gibraltar to be now unluckily taken,* still, according to the noble Lord's own doctrine, it would be no great matter. For although we are not masters of the sea at present, we probably shall be so some time or other, and then, my Lords, there will be no difficulty in retaking Gibraltar." N.B. This Earl is a privy counsellor, and appeared to have concerted this satisfactory answer with Peg Trentham at the fire-side.

2. Sir Edward Hawke, on Wednesday last, gave the House of Commons a very pompous account of the fleet. Being asked why, if our navy was so numerous and ready for service, a squadron was not sent to Gibraltar and the West Indies? his answer was candid:—"That for his part he did not understand sending ships abroad when, for aught he knew, they might be wanted to defend our own coast." Such is the care taken of our possessions abroad! One great minister tells us they may be easily retaken; another assures us that they cannot be defended. Will that man who sleepeth never awake until destruction comes upon him? Has he no friend, no servant, to draw his curtain, until Troy is actually in flames?

3. Lord North informed the House of Commons on Wednesday that, although he wished for an honourable accommodation, he thought it his duty to tell the House, that he feared *war was too probable;* that he intended to move for a further augmentation of ten thousand seamen, and that, at any rate, he should advise the keeping up the naval and military force upon the augmented establishment, for that, notwithstanding the language held by the French and Spanish ministers, there was, all over France and Spain, the greatest appearance of hostile preparations.

4. The riot in the House of Lords has shocked the delicacy of Sir Fletcher Norton. Upon occasion of some clamour yesterday, he called to them, with all the softness of a bassoon, *Pray, gentlemen, be orderly; you are almost as bad as the other House.*

5. On Tuesday last, Lord Camden delivered into the House of Lords a paper containing three questions, relative to the doctrine laid down in Lord Mansfield's paper, which he desired that Lord would answer, if he could. Lord Mansfield was very angry at being taken by surprise upon a subject he had never had an opportunity of considering, and said that he valued the constitutional liberty of the subject too much to *answer interrogatories.*

THOMAS HUTCHINSON TO LORD HILLS-BOROUGH (1771).

Source.—*Calendar of Home Office Papers, 1770-1772.* Pp. 191-193.

Home Office Papers

Thos. Hutchinson, Governor of [Massachusetts Bay], to Lord [Hillsborough].

22 Jan.—The disorders in the colonies do not seem to have been caused by the defects in the forms or constitutions of government. They have not prevailed in proportion as one has been under a more popular form of government than another. They must be attributed to a cause, common to all the colonies,—a loose, false, and absurd notion of the nature of government, spread by designing, artful men, setting bounds to the supreme authority, and admitting parts of the community, and even individuals, to judge when those bounds are exceeded, and to obey or disobey accordingly. These principles prevailing, there can be no interior force exerted, and disorder and confusion must be the effect; and when there is no apprehension of force from the supreme authority, the effect is the same in the distinct parts as in the whole. Under these circumstances measures for reforming the constitution of any people will probably be ineffectual, and tend to increase their disorders. The colonies were under these circumstances when he wrote his first private letter. There was a general opinion prevailing that they could distress the kingdom by withdrawing their commerce from it, and that there was not the least danger of any compulsory measures. In this colony there was room to hope for a change of circumstances, but it was uncertain, and probably at a distance. They had just felt the shock of that most fortunate stroke which freed the Castle from any dependence upon the people, and kept the harbour and town of Boston under the command of the King's ships; but the effects did not appear. He was striving for a just decision in the case of the soldiers, and not without hope, but far from being certain of success. There was a prospect of the dissolution of the confederacies against importation, though several of the colonies appeared to be more resolute. There was also an expectation of a rupture between Great Britain and France or Spain, or both, which would tend to show the people their dependence on the kingdom, and the reasonableness of their submission to the supreme authority. He was not insensible of the peculiar defects in the constitution of this province, and he has complained of the Council as being under undue influence, and casting their weight into that scale which had much too great proportion before; but was doubtful himself, and there were others doubtful also, whether, while the body of the people continued in the state they were then in, councillors appointed by the Crown would dare to undertake the trust; or, if they should do it, whether the people in general would not refuse to submit to their authority; and he feared the consequences of either would more than countervail the advantages to arise merely from an alteration in the constitution. To this must be attributed the want of determination which appeared in his private letters, and not to any unwillingness to trust his Lordship with his real sentiments.

The change in the temper of the people has been brought about sooner, and to a greater degree, than anybody could expect; and they seem now to be as well prepared to receive such a change in the constitution as at any future time; or, if it should be deferred, they will probably remain in tolerably good order until such time as may be judged convenient, provided something is done in the meantime to discover the resentment of the kingdom against their avowed principles and practices, which shall give them cause to imagine that further measures are to be taken with them. Such resentment has been everywhere expected. If omitted, they will go back to their former disorders. That wise step of changing the garrison at the Castle began their cure. In the height of this confusion a citadel upon Fort Hill seemed also to be necessary. Now thinks the same end is answered without it. It may, however, be proper for the King to have the actual possession of the spot, either by erecting a warehouse or magazine, or by making some kind of enclosure to restrain encroachments, and yet not prevent the inhabitants from using the place to walk and air themselves in; as they now frequently do. There is a vote of the town for selling it. Will watch their motions, and, if anything further is attempted, will take public notice of it. If no further advances are made for securing good behaviour, there certainly will be no receding. To depart suddenly from what has been done at the Castle, &c., would be very dangerous. Every Act of Parliament carried into execution in the colonies tends to strengthen Government there. A firm persuasion that Parliament is determined at all events to maintain the supreme authority is all they want; few or none are so weak as to question the power to do it. If Acts were passed more or less to control them every Session, they would soon be familiarized to them; their erroneous opinions would die away, and peace and order would revive. An Act to enable the King to alter the bounds of the province by his commission, the charter notwithstanding, by making the province of Main, and country east of it, a distinct and separate province, and to annex or not, as His Majesty should think fit, New Hampshire to the Massachusetts, or to separate the country east of Penobscot and annex it to Nova Scotia, might either be kept as a rod over them, or, if executed immediately, would show a just resentment against the province for countenancing the intrusions in the eastern country, whereby the King's timber is exposed to waste and havoc, and would be a striking instance of the power and authority of Parliament. Gives his reasons for thinking that the Act would be executed. Suggests that whenever the charter and case of the province comes under consideration, instead of expressly declaring that the power of electing councillors by the Assembly shall determine, the King should be enabled by his Royal order of declaration to determine it, and to appoint a Council instead, as he shall think proper. The late Act permitting the issue of bills of credit at New

York was extremely well adapted to maintain the authority of Parliament.

Makes application in behalf of Capt. Phillips, the late commanding officer, who is by far the greatest sufferer of any belonging to the late garrison.

Is taking every measure, consistent with the honour of Government, to reconcile civil and military, whigs and tories. They begin to be sensible that it must be a very bad constitution indeed which is not preferable to the savage state they have been in for some years past.—Boston. Private. R. 30th March.

Thos. Hutchinson, Governor of [Massachusetts Bay], to [Lord Hillsborough].

25 Aug.—Mr. Henry Barnes, who lately arrived from England, has requested him, the Governor, to cover a letter from him to his Lordship, and to represent his sufferings and services in the cause of Government. Has not been made acquainted with the contents of the letter. Mr. Barnes has certainly suffered greatly by refusing to comply with the scheme of non-importation, and by his endeavours to support the authority of the magistrate; but in his solicitations for compensation he shows more impatience than could be wished. Is willing to attribute it to a mind chafed with his troubles, and impressed with a strong sense of his merit, which he supposes to exceed that of many others who have received the favours of Government. He complains of his, the Governor's, neglecting him, in not particularly recommending his case when he went to England. Though he did not ask it, he yet concluded it had been done in the course of public correspondence. He, the Governor, transmitted an account of the incendiary letters, and would have been more particular had he been requested. Thought that for his general character, which is very good, he depended on Sir Francis Barnard, who held him in esteem, and to whom he was more particularly known. If there were anything in the province in his, the Governor's, disposal worth accepting, would give it him, but there is not.

Makes his grateful acknowledgments to his Lordship for H.M.'s warrant to the Commissioners of the Customs for the payment of his salary. The fund on which the warrant is charged would rise to a very large sum if the illicit trade with Holland could be prevented.

The consumption of tea in America exceeds what anybody in England imagines. Some suppose five-sixths of the consumption in the last two years has been smuggled, and in Philadelphia and New York it is judged nine-tenths. The traders make such an extravagant profit that it will require more frequent seizures to discourage them than there is any reason to hope for. If the India Company had continued the sale of their teas at 2s. 2d. to 2s. 4d., as they sold them two years ago, the Dutch trade would have been over by this time; but now that teas are 3s. and upwards in England, the illicit trader can afford to lose one chest in three, whereas not one in a hundred has been seized. The custom-house officers on shore have strong inducements to do their duty, being entitled to a proportion of one-third or more, but they are really afraid of the rage of the people. The sea officers have of late been more active, and Admiral Montague appears disposed to keep out his cruisers. Doubts, however, whether this trade will ever be discouraged in any other way than by reducing the price in England to the exporter very near the price it is at in Holland. For want of this, the revenue has lost, the last and present years, at least 60,000*l.* sterling, from the 3d. duty only. Believes the cruisers are capable of doing more. Suggests that a greater proportion is necessary for the particular officer who makes the seizure under a commission from the Customs than what he is now entitled to. Has discovered, when he has sworn some of the Navy officers to qualify them for their commissions from the Customs, a great indifference and disinclination to make themselves obnoxious to the people without any great advantage to themselves.—Boston. R. 29th Oct.

Thos. Hutchinson, Governor of [Massachusetts Bay], to Lord [Hillsborough].

10 Sept.—In reply to his Lordship's private letter of 30 May, not received till he had closed his letter of the 25th August. Now submits an estimate of the consumption of Bohea tea in America. The two towns of Boston and Charlestown consume a chest, or about 340 lbs., per day. The towns are not more than one-eighth, perhaps not more than one-tenth of the province. Suppose they consume only 300 chests in the year, and allow that they are one-eighth, it will make 2,400 chests for the whole province. This is much short, for in the country towns there is much more tea drunk in proportion than at Boston. This province is not one-eighth part of the colonies; and in other Governments, New York especially, they consume tea in much greater proportion. If it be one-eighth, the whole continent consumes 19,200 chests, which at 4*l.* per chest, the 3d. duty only, amounts to 76,800*l.* But the computation is short in every part. In New York they import scarce any other than Dutch teas. In Rhode Island and Pennsylvania it is little better. In this province the Dutch traders are increasing. Has frequent information of large quantities when too late; and sometimes such persons are concerned as he thought could not have been capable of countenancing perjury or fraud. Cannot help repeating that unless the East India Company bring the price of tea so near to the price in Holland as to make the profit of importing from thence not equal to the risk, there will scarce be any imported from England. The acting collector at Falmouth, in Casco Bay, acknowledged it to be true that the Acts of Trade were broken every day in his district, but said the officers on shore could not prevent it. He suggested that the only way to prevent it was to increase the number of small schooners, and to keep one or more constantly cruising in the bay, rigged and fitted like schooners. "We have not virtue enough to become obnoxious to the people merely from a sense of duty." It seems, therefore, best to have one officer only in each vessel with a commission from the Customs, and he to have the command, and to be entitled to all but the King's half of the forfeiture; which would give him a good chance of making a small fortune. There does not seem to be the same reason for sharing any part among the crew or other officers as in cases of prizes taken in war, where all their lives are exposed; for in the present case there is no danger of resistance to an armed vessel, seeing that all the smugglers are themselves unarmed and depend entirely on concealment.—Boston. R. 29 October.

REFORMERS IN PARLIAMENT RECOM-MENDED TO SINK DIFFERENCES AND PRO-MOTE UNION (1771).

Source.—*Letters of Junius* (Letter LIX.). London: G. Bell and Sons. 1910. Vol. i.

Letters of Junius

To the Printer of the "Public Advertiser," October 5, 1771.

Sir,

No man laments more sincerely than I do the unhappy differences which have arisen among the friends of the people, and divided them from each other. The cause undoubtedly suffers as well by the diminution of that strength which union carries with it as by the separate loss of personal reputation, which every man sustains when his character and conduct are frequently held forth in odious or contemptible colours. These differences are only advantageous to the common enemy of the country; the hearty friends of the cause are provoked and disgusted; the lukewarm advocate avails himself of any pretence to relapse into that indolent indifference about everything that ought to interest an Englishman, so unjustly dignified with the title of moderation; the false, insidious partisan, who creates or foments the disorder, sees the fruit of his dishonest industry ripen beyond his hopes, and rejoices in the promise of a banquet, only delicious to such an appetite as his own. It is time for those who really mean the *cause* and the *people*, who have no view to private advantage, and who have virtue enough to prefer the general good of the community to the gratification of personal animosities,—it is time for such men to interpose; let us try whether these fatal dissensions may not yet be reconciled; or, if that be impracticable, let us guard at least against the worst effects of division, and endeavour to persuade these furious partisans, if they will not consent to draw together, to be separately useful to that cause which they all pretend to be attached to. Honour and honesty must not be renounced, although a thousand modes of right and wrong were to occupy the degrees of morality between Zeno and Epicurus. The fundamental principles of Christianity may still be preserved, though every zealous sectary adheres to his own exclusive doctrine, and pious ecclesiastics make it part of their religion to persecute one another. The civil constitution, too, that legal liberty, that general creed, which every Englishman professes, may still be supported, though Wilkes and Horne, Townshend and Sawbridge, should obstinately refuse to communicate; and even if the fathers of the church, if Savile, Richmond, Camden, Rockingham, and Chatham, should disagree in the ceremonies of their political worship, and even in the interpretation of twenty texts in Magna Charta. I speak to the people as one of the people. Let us employ these men in whatever departments their various abilities are best suited to, and as much to the advantage of the common cause as their different inclinations will permit. They cannot serve *us* without essentially serving themselves.

If Mr. Nash be elected, he will hardly venture, after so recent a mark of the personal esteem of his fellow-citizens, to declare himself immediately a courtier. The spirit and activity of the sheriffs will, I hope, be sufficient to counteract any sinister intentions of the lord mayor; in collision with *their* virtue, perhaps he may take fire.

It is not necessary to exact from Mr. Wilkes the virtues of a Stoic. *They* were inconsistent with themselves who, almost at the same moment, represented him as the basest of mankind, yet seemed to expect from him such instances of fortitude and self-denial as would do honour to an apostle; it is not, however, flattery to say, that he is obstinate, intrepid, and fertile in expedients; that he has no possible resource but in the public favour, is, in my judgment, a considerable recommendation of him. I wish that every man who pretended to popularity were in the same predicament; I wish that a retreat to St. James's were not so easy and open as patriots have found it. To Mr. Wilkes there is no access. However he may be misled by passion or imprudence, I think he cannot be guilty of a deliberate treachery to the public; the favour of his country constitutes the shield which defends him against a thousand daggers, desertion would disarm him....

I have too much respect for the abilities of Mr. Horne to flatter myself that these gentlemen will ever be cordially reunited; it is not, however, unreasonable to expect that each of them should act his separate part with honour and integrity to the public. As for differences of opinion upon speculative questions, if we wait until *they* are reconciled, the action of human affairs must be suspended for ever. But neither are we to look for perfection in any one man, nor for agreement among many. When Lord Chatham affirms that the authority of the British legislature is not supreme over the colonies in the same sense in which it is supreme over Great Britain; when Lord Camden supposes a necessity (which the king is to judge of), and, founded upon that necessity, attributes to the crown a legal power (not given by the Act itself) to suspend the operation of an act of the legislature, I listen to them both with diffidence and respect, but without the smallest degree of conviction or assent; yet I doubt not they delivered their real sentiments, nor ought they to be hastily condemned. I, *too*, have a claim to the candid interpretation of my country, when I acknowledge an involuntary compulsive assent to one very unpopular opinion. I lament the unhappy necessity, whenever it arises, of providing for the safety of the state by a temporary invasion of the personal liberty of the subject. Would to God it were practicable to reconcile these important objects in every possible situation of public affairs! I regard the legal liberty of the meanest man in Britain as much as my own, and would defend it with the same zeal. I know we must stand or fall together. But I never can doubt that the community has a right to command, as well as to purchase, the service of its members. I see that right founded originally upon a necessity which supersedes all argument; I see it established by usage immemorial, and admitted by more than a tacit assent of the legislature. I conclude there is no remedy in the nature of things for the grievance complained of; for if there were, it must long since have been redressed. Though numberless opportunities have presented themselves highly favourable to public liberty, no successful attempt has ever been made for the relief of the subject in this article. Yet it has been felt and complained of ever since England had a navy. The conditions which constitute this right must be taken together; separately, they have little weight. It is not fair to argue from any abuse in the execution to the illegality of the power, much less is a conclusion to be drawn from the navy to the land service. A seaman can never be employed but against the enemies of his country. The only case in which the king can have a right to arm his subjects in general is that of a foreign force being actually landed upon our coast. Whenever that case happens, no true Englishman will inquire whether the king's right to compel him to defend his country be the custom of England or a grant of the legislature. With regard to the press for seamen, it does not follow that the symptoms may not be softened, although the distemper cannot be cured. Let bounties be increased as far as the public purse can support them.[5] Still they have a limit, and when every reasonable expense is incurred, it will be found, in fact, that the spur of the press is wanted to give operation to the bounty.

Upon the whole, I never had a doubt about the strict right of pressing, until I heard that Lord Mansfield had applauded Lord Chatham for delivering something like this doctrine in the House of Lords. That consideration staggered me not a little. But, upon reflection, his conduct accounts naturally for itself. He knew the doctrine was unpopular, and was eager to fix it upon the man who is the first object of his fear and detestation. The cunning Scotchman never speaks truth without a fraudulent design. In council he generally affects to take a moderate part. Besides his natural timidity, it makes part of his political plan never to be known to recommend violent measures. When the guards are called forth to murder their fellow-subjects, it is not by the ostensible advice of Lord Mansfield. That odious office, his prudence tells him, is better left to such men as Gower and Weymouth, as Barrington and Grafton. Lord Hillsborough wisely confines *his* firmness to the distant Americans. The designs of Mansfield are more subtle, more effectual, and secure.—Who attacks the liberty of the press?—Lord Mansfield. Who invades the constitutional power of juries?—Lord Mansfield. What judge ever challenged a juryman, but Lord Mansfield? Who was that judge, who, to save the king's brother, affirmed that a man of the first rank and quality, who obtains a verdict in a suit for criminal conversation, is entitled to no greater damages than the meanest mechanic?—Lord Mansfield? Who is it makes commissioners of the great seal?—Lord Mansfield? Who is it forms a decree for those commissioners, deciding against Lord Chatham,[6] and afterwards (finding himself opposed by the judges) declares in Parliament that he never had a doubt that the law was in direct opposition to

[5] This suggestion was adopted by the cities of London, Bristol, and Edinburgh, and the towns of Montrose, Aberdeen, Campbeltown, and Lynn.

[6] On the Burton Pynsent estate, which was disputed by the relatives of the deceased with the Earl of Chatham.

that decree?—Lord Mansfield. Who is he that has made it the study and practice of his life to undermine and alter the whole system of jurisprudence in the Court of King's Bench?—Lord Mansfield. There never existed a man but himself who answered exactly to so complicated a description. Compared to these enormities, his original attachment to the Pretender (to whom his dearest brother was confidential secretary) is a virtue of the first magnitude. But the hour of impeachment *will* come, and neither he nor Grafton shall escape me. Now let them make common cause against England and the House of Hanover. A Stuart and a Murray should sympathize with each other.

When I refer to signal instances of unpopular opinions delivered and maintained by men who may well be supposed to have no view but the public good, I do not mean to renew the discussion of such opinions. I should be sorry to revive the dormant questions of *Stamp Act, Corn Bill,* or *Press Warrant.* I mean only to illustrate one useful proposition, which it is the intention of this paper to inculcate:—*That we should not generally reject the friendship or services of any man because he differs from us in a particular opinion.* This will not appear a superfluous caution if we observe the ordinary conduct of mankind. In public affairs, there is the least chance of a perfect concurrence of sentiment or inclination. Yet every man is able to contribute something to the common stock, and no man's contribution should be rejected. If individuals have no virtues, their vices may be of use to us. I care not with what principle the new-born patriot is animated, if the measures he supports are beneficial to the community. The nation is interested in his conduct. His motives are his own. The properties of a patriot are perishable in the individual, but there is a quick succession of subjects, and the breed is worth preserving. The spirit of the Americans may be an useful example to us. Our dogs and horses are English only upon English ground; but patriotism, it seems, may be improved by transplanting. I will not reject a bill which tends to confine parliamentary privilege within reasonable bounds, though it should be stolen from the House of Cavendish, and introduced by Mr. Onslow. The features of the infant are a proof of the descent, and vindicate the noble birth from the baseness of the adoption. I willingly accept of a sarcasm from Colonel Barré, or a simile from Mr. Burke. Even the silent vote of Mr. Calcraft is worth reckoning in a division. What though he riots in the plunder of the army, and has only determined to be a patriot when he could not be a peer? Let us profit by the assistance of such men while they are with us, and place them, if it be possible, in the post of danger, to prevent desertion. The wary Wedderburne, the pompous Suffolk, never threw away the scabbard, nor ever went upon a forlorn hope. They always treated the king's servants as men with whom, some time or other, they might possibly be in friendship. When a man who stands forth for the public has gone that length from which there is no practicable retreat, when he has given that kind of personal offence, which a pious monarch never pardons, I then begin to think him in earnest, and that he never will have occasion to solicit the forgiveness of his country. But instances of a determination so entire and unreserved are rarely met with. Let us take mankind *as they are.* Let us distribute the virtues and abilities of individuals according to the offices they affect, and, when they quit the service, let us endeavour to supply their places with better men than we have lost. In this country there are always candidates enough for popular favour. The temple of *fame* is the shortest passage to riches and preferment.

Above all things, let me guard my countrymen against the meanness and folly of accepting of a trifling or moderate compensation for extraordinary and essential injuries. Our enemies treat us as the cunning trader does the unskilful Indian. They magnify their generosity when they give us baubles, of little proportionate value, for ivory and gold. The same House of Commons, who robbed the constituent body of their right of free election; who presumed to *make* a law under pretence of *declaring* it; who paid our good king's debts, without once inquiring how they were incurred; who gave thanks for repeated murders committed at home, and for national infamy incurred abroad; who screened Lord Mansfield; who imprisoned the magistrates of the metropolis for asserting the subject's right to the protection of the laws; who erased a judicial record, and ordered all proceedings in a criminal suit to be suspended;—this very House of Commons have graciously consented that their own members may be compelled to pay their debts, and that contested elections shall for the future be determined with some decent regard to the merits of the case. The event of the suit is of no consequence to the crown. While parliaments are septennial, the purchase of the sitting member or of the petitioner makes but the difference of a day. Concessions such as these are of little moment to the sum of things; unless it be to prove that the worst of men are sensible of the injuries they have done us, and perhaps to demonstrate to us the imminent danger of our situation. In the shipwreck of the state, trifles float and are preserved, while everything solid and valuable sinks to the bottom, and is lost for ever.

Junius.

DISTRESS CAUSED BY HIGH PRICES (1772).

Source.—*Calendar of Home Office Papers, 1770-1772.* P. 479.

Home Office Papers

Forestalling and Engrossing.

11 April.—A paper signed "near Dorchester," addressed to the King (the newspapers taking notice of His Majesty's desire to see the price of provisions lowered), to lay before him the evils of forestalling and engrossing. As examples of engrossing in the neighbourhood of Dorchester, the writer instances the manors of Came, Whitcomb, Muncton, and Bockhampton. The first, he says, about thirty years before, had many inhabitants, many holding leasehold estates under the lord of the manor for three lives. Some of these had estates of 15*l.*, 20*l.*, and 30*l.* a year, being for the most part careful, industrious people, obliged to be careful to keep a little cash in order to keep the estate in the family if a life should drop. Their corn was brought to market, and they were content with the market price. Their cattle were sold in the same manner. Their children when of proper age were married, and children begotten, without fear of poverty. But the lord had since turned out all the people, and the whole place was in his own hands, while not half the quantity of corn was sown that formerly had been. The writer also gives an account how one Wm. Taunton, though only a tenant of the Dean and Chapter of Exon, was gradually getting the whole parish into his own hands. He says, comparing his own with past times, that formerly a farmer that occupied 100*l.* a year was thought a tolerable one, and he that occupied four or five hundred pounds a very great one indeed; but now they had farmers that occupied from one thousand to two thousand per annum, who did not want money to pay their rent, as did the little farmers, who were obliged to sell their corn, &c. The writer gives it as the general opinion that the kingdom had become greatly depopulated, some averring the population to have decreased by a fourth within the preceding hundred years. He further says: "Your Majesty must put a stop to inclosures, or oblige yᵉ lord of yᵉ manor to keep up yᵉ antient custom of it, and not suffer him to buy his tenant's interest; to have all the houses pulled down, and yᵉ whole parish turn'd into a farm: this is a fashionable practice, and by none more yⁿ Jnᵒ Damer, Esq., yᵉ owner of Came, and his brother Lord Milton."

MEETINGS OF WEAVERS AND OTHERS TO PETITION THE KING (1773).

Source.—*Calendar of Home Office Papers, 1773-1775.* Pp. 39-42, and
65.

Home Office Papers

13-27 April.—A series of letters and other papers about meetings of weavers, coalheavers, &c. A printed handbill, calling them together, was first dispersed in Spitalfields on the 12th April. Next day notice of it was given to Lord Rochford by Sir John Fielding. The handbill to the weavers is signed "Ten Thousand," and exhorts them "to stand up and carry the truth to the King." "Let us rise up as one man and wait humbly upon the King at St. James' every day. He will then grant the humble petition of the worthy Lord Mayor and liverymen of London, who have begged him to have pity upon the poor, and to remove those evil ministers who will not lower the price of provisions to relieve us, and who will take no care of our trade. Let us go daily and repeat our prayer to the King, and he will at length hearken to us, and remove his evil counsellors. Then shall we and our poor families be able to gain an honest and comfortable livelihood by a reasonable industry; if not, our trade will be lost for ever. We all remember that some years ago more than 20,000 of our trade waited on the King for several days together, and he was convinced of their distress. N.B.—Do not be guilty of any disorder; only show yourselves to the King, that he may see your distress every day."

The magistrates in Bethnal Green granted a privy search-warrant, to "set aside all tumults and riots which might happen," and next day reported that everything had been quiet the night before.

On the 16th April it was reported that printed handbills, verbatim the same as those to the weavers, except the address [and the signature, "One of Two Thousand"] had been distributed among the coalheavers in Shadwell. Everything was quiet, but (say the justices) "we greatly fear some evil agents are abroad sowing sedition."

On the 17th April Mr. Justice Wilmot acquainted Lord Suffolk that everything was quiet among the Spitalfields weavers, but that he was afraid the City Marshal was making himself "too busy" among them. Their intention then was to rise in a body on the 26th and proceed to the House of Commons. The sworn information of a victualler in Bethnal Green states that the City Marshal came to his house to inquire into the grievances of the weavers, that it was agreed that eight or ten men should meet at the informant's house to present a petition to the Lord Mayor; but on his objecting to this proposal, the City Marshal desired them to meet at any place they thought proper, or come into the city, and he would protect them, and assured them my Lord Mayor would serve them so long as they kept peace and good order. The Lord Mayor's account is that he sent the City Marshal with the Sheriffs into Spitalfields, and that the former got himself introduced the same evening to about 50 weavers, when, the handbill distributed the day before becoming the subject of conversation, he expostulated with them on the imprudence and danger of such a proceeding, and convinced them it must have been some enemy to their well-being who had suggested it. The City Marshal's account convinced the Lord Mayor that the intention of assembling did not originate with the weavers. The Lord Mayor encloses a letter from "A Citizen," in a disguised hand, in which the hope is expressed that his Lordship, now that the people had become the "messengers of their own distress," would not use his authority to interpose "any unnecessary obstruction to the miserable people," the success of his own endeavours for the service of his country not having proved equal to the "honourable part" he had acted, and the "late remonstrance" having been "treated with a contempt which nothing but a persuasion of its falsity could justify." In order to discover the origin of the hand-bills, Sir John Fielding suggested that they should be shown to printers who might learn something from the type, he himself having once been very successful in discovering the forgery of a banknote by an application to the copper-plate printers, who detected it to have been done by a gun engraver. He also advised the offer of a reward from the justices at Hicks' Hall.

On the 23rd April Mr. Justice Wilmot wrote from the Globe Tavern in Moorfields that he had just received the handbill which he enclosed, in consequence of which he had come to Moorfields. He found 300 or 400 weavers gathered, "and by their coming in it's likely there will be thousands." The body of the handbill is in the same terms as those already referred to, but addressed in this case to the "poor watermen, porters, and carmen, and their families, &c.," and signed "Two Thousand." There is the same postscript deprecating disorder. A similar handbill was also distributed, addressed to the weavers as before. On this occasion the Lord Mayor, being applied to, quitted his chair at the Old Bailey, took a hackney coach, and went to the scene to disperse the mob. Before he reached the spot, however, the "three or four hundred weavers" who had assembled had quietly dispersed. It was Mr. Justice Sherwood who succeeded in getting the crowd to disperse on this occasion. He went alone to Moorfields. The weavers could not tell him what they had come together for. Their only complaint was that they had a bill before the House of Commons which they were afraid would not pass. He promised to convey any application they had to make to the King or the Ministry, a promise which they cheerfully accepted, and then immediately dispersed.

The night before Mr. Alderman Oliver had received a letter in a large feigned hand from "A Citizen," intimating that nothing was intended but that the poor people should go in large bodies to convey that conviction which every gentler method had been so repeatedly yet so vainly tried to produce, and asking him "if a body of starving people" should be found assembling in Moorfields, in order to be under the protection of the city magistrates to consult how to make their sorrows known to their Sovereign, not to let them be hunted by the ill-timed zeal of the neighbouring justices who might apply for his assistance in suppressing a disturbance when the only design was to excite the emotions of humanity in favour of the wretched. For the discovery of the writer of this letter and of the one to the Lord Mayor, already referred to, a reward of 100*l*. was offered, with a pardon to an accomplice.

On the same day (23rd April) Mr. Robert Pell, chairman of the Tower Sessions, wrote that after diligent secret inquiry after the printed handbills said to have been distributed among the coalheavers in the Tower division, he had been induced to believe that their distribution, if real, had not been general. He had within the last few days, however, noticed a person (for some time in the commission of the peace for the county, but whose name had been struck out on account of certain transactions with the riotous coalheavers) in better plight as to garb and outward appearances than he had been seen in since his disgrace, and in close familiar conference with labouring people in the streets of the neighbourhood. Upon this man he said he had set a watch. In this letter is a printed petition signed by several persons, whose places of residence are also given, addressed "To the nobility, gentry, &c. who are real lovers of the King and country's prosperity," attributing the distresses of the silkweavers to the great encouragement given to the importation and wearing of foreign wrought silks, and imploring their assistance to discountenance such "impolitic and unnatural" practices by refusing to wear or purchase such goods.

On 24th April Sir John Fielding proposed that the magistrates of each division should sit for a week every morning from 8 till 11, having the high constable and all the petty constables stationed near them with proper messengers to reconnoitre and inquire. He thought that nothing else would counteract the endeavours which were being made to disturb the public peace by inviting ignorant and illiterate bodies to assemble. He mentioned the plan to "avoid different opinions in the magistrates, and that the whole might be uniform and the force united." Monday, Thursday, and Friday were the particular days of apprehension. As the general constables were men of business, and must necessarily lose much time in the execution of this plan, he suggested that Sir John Hawkins should be authorised to make them amends.

The weavers were summoned to meet again on Monday, 26th April, when they were promised they should "absolutely see a petition to be delivered to His Majesty's person by the hands of people who have no reason to be ashamed or afraid to appear in behalf of such distress." Mr. Wilmot, Mr. Sherwood, and Mr. Pell proceeded to Moorfields, the place of meeting. After a conference with a posse of about 200 weavers they succeeded in getting possession of the proposed petition, which was "artfully drawn up," and then retired to a public-house while the weavers elected a committee of six or eight to meet them. These made certain proposals to the magistrates, who gave an answer next day which thoroughly satisfied the committee, who sincerely promised on behalf of their body to have no more irregular meetings on the magistrates' engaging to consider of some mode of subjecting their wages to the decision of the magistrates in their quarter sessions.

Sir John Fielding to the Earl of Suffolk.

9 July.—Assisted yesterday at the Middlesex General Quarter Sessions to carry into execution the late Act of Parliament for regulating the wages of journeymen weavers in Spitalfields, &c.; and the wages were then settled by a numerous and unanimous Bench to the entire satisfaction of those masters and journeymen weavers who appeared there. I sincerely hope this step will prove a radical cure for all tumultuous assemblies from that quarter. By this statute your Lordship has conveyed contentment to the minds of thousands of His Majesty's subjects. The Act for appointing clergymen with proper salaries to attend the gaols, according to my proposals, was also carried into execution. This preventive step will, I am persuaded be attended with very salutary effects. I hope your Lordship will take advantage of my Lord North's leisure to settle the affair regarding my preventive plan now lying before him for His Majesty's approbation.

DESTRUCTION OF TEA (CARGOES) AT BOS-TON (DECEMBER, 1773).

Source.—*Calendar of Home Office Papers (1773-1775). Pp. 175 et seq.*

Home Office Papers

Lords of the Admiralty to the Earl of Dartmouth.

27 Jan.—Enclosing a copy of another letter from Rear-Admiral Montague, dated at Boston, the 17th Dec. last, give an account of a mob having assembled and destroyed the tea exported from England by the East India Company.—Admiralty Office.

The enclosure. On the evening of 16 Dec., between 6 and 7 o'clock, a large mob assembled with axes, &c., encouraged by Mr. John Hancock, Samuel Adams, and others, and marched in a body to where the ships lay, and there destroyed the whole by starting it into the sea. During the whole of this transaction neither the Governor, Magistrates, owners, nor Revenue officers ever called for the Admiral's assistance. If they had, he could easily have prevented the execution of the plan, but must have endangered the lives of many innocent people by firing on the town.

Lord Viscount Barrington to the Earl of Dartmouth.

28 Jan.—Enclosing copies of two letters from Lieut.-Col. Leslie, commanding the 64th Regiment at Castle William, Boston.—War Office.

The enclosures, dated respectively the 6th and 17th Dec., 1773. In the first Col. Leslie says that the four Commissioners of the Custom-house and the five tea agents had taken refuge with him that day week, and were likely to continue some time. The Governor had not mentioned any desire of marching the regiment to town. Only two of the tea ships had then arrived, and Mr. Hancock, "the Governor's Captain of his Cadet Company," was mounting guard on board them, to prevent the landing of that part of the cargo, "a most daring insult to his Excellency." In the second letter he states that the Sons of Liberty had destroyed 340 chests of tea that lay altogether at one of the wharfs. The fourth vessel was stranded near to Cape Cod; but the tea was got safe on shore, and it was expected it had shared the same fate as the last. The regiment was ready, had it been called upon. The Council would not agree to the troops going to town. "However, it must end in that. Lenity won't do now with the people here." The gentlemen who had taken refuge in Castle William still continued there.

Chairman of the East India Company to Lord Dartmouth.

? *29 Jan.*—Transmitting copies of several papers lately received relative to the tea affair in America.—East India House, Saturday night.

The enclosures; viz., (*b*) Petition from the Company's agents in Boston (Richard Clarke and Sons, Benjamin Faneuil, jun., and Thos. and Elisha Hutchinson) to the Governor and Council; and minutes of the meetings of the Council held thereupon.

(*c*) Letters from the agents to the Directors of the East India Company, dated Castle William, near Boston, respectively the 2nd and 9th Dec. 1773.

(*d*) Letters from the Company's agents (Roger Smith and Leger and Greenwood) at Charlestown, South Carolina, dated respectively 4 and 18 Dec. 1773.

(*e*) Letter from the Boston agents to the Directors, dated Castle William, 17 Dec. 1773.

The Boston agents petitioned the Governor and Council to take charge of the tea on its arrival. The meetings of the Council when this petition was taken into consideration were several times adjourned between 19 and 29 Nov. Finally, on the latter date a committee of Council, consisting of James Bowdoin, Samuel Dexter, and John Winthrop, Esq., having been previously appointed to draw up a report of the debate, to be presented to the Governor, their report was discussed and accepted. It described the origin of the disturbances to be the Act laying a duty upon tea in America, and, in regard to the petition, referred the petitioners for personal protection to the justices of the peace, and declared they had no authority to take the tea, or any other merchandise, out of the agent's care, while, if they advised the landing of it, the duty would have to be paid or secured, and they would therefore be advising a measure inconsistent with the declared sentiments of both Houses in the last winter session of the General Court, advice which they considered to be altogether inexpedient and improper. They said they had seen with regret some late disturbances, and had advised the prosecution of their authors. The letters of the agents give an account of the people's proceedings, and that they themselves had been obliged to take refuge in Castle William. The letter of 17 Dec. announces the destruction of the tea.

In Charlestown, after several meetings of the townspeople, it was decided that the teas should not be allowed to be landed, whilst six months was allowed to consume the teas then on hand, after which time no teas were to be used on any pretence whilst the duty payable in America continued.

WAR MATERIAL FOR AMERICA (1774).

Source.—*Calendar of Home Office Papers (1773-1775). Pp. 240 et seq.*

Home Office Papers

Earl of Suffolk to the Earl of Dartmouth.

31 Aug.—Sends extracts from two letters from Sir Joseph Yorke relative to large quantities of gunpowder said to be purchased in Holland and shipped for some of the ports in North America.—St. James's.

The enclosures. It was the house of Crommelin at Amsterdam which was chiefly concerned in this trade. A great quantity of war material was exported by the Dutch to St. Eustatia, the centre of all contraband in that part of the world.

Earl of Suffolk to the Earl of Dartmouth.

24 Sept.—Giving notice of intelligence received from Sir Joseph Yorke that it was being confirmed to his Excellency more and more every day that North America is largely supplied by way of St. Eustatia with what it does not choose to take from England, or to export directly from Holland, in which the Dutch find their account and will not let the market want.—St. James's.

Earl of Suffolk to the Earl of Dartmouth.

25 Oct.—Enclosing an extract from a letter from Sir Joseph Yorke, stating the steps taken by him in consequence of the instructions transmitted to him by messenger on the 17th instant.—St. James's.

The enclosure. Sir Joseph found the Pensionary as well disposed to satisfy the King as the most zealous wishes could expect. He said that whatever depended upon him to stop such a dangerous traffic should be done, though the manner of doing it could not be immediately determined, because it might not be advisable to exert an extraordinary power which might occasion both a clamour and alarm. He explained, in conversation, that in the present temper of the magistracy of Amsterdam it would be difficult for the Ministry at the Hague to work at all through that channel. He imagined that the channel of the Admiralty at Amsterdam, which is at the same time charged with the department of the Customs, might be preferred. Afterwards saw M. Fagel, whose attachment and zeal are too well known to require any new assurances. He soon brought a letter to M. Boreel, Fiscal of the Admiralty, and said the Prince did not think it necessary or advisable to use any extraordinary methods, but that he had desired M. Boreel to examine strictly into the affair, to prevent in every way the departure of any vessel with such a cargo, &c. Calling on the Prince to thank him in the King's name, the Prince said he should always contribute with joy to the ease and welfare of His Majesty and his dominions, but that he, Sir Joseph, knew the merchants well enough to be convinced they would sell arms and ammunition to besiege Amsterdam itself.

Lords of the Admiralty to the Earl of Dartmouth.

9 Dec.—Send copies of letters of 1st and 11 Nov. and 6th inst. from Lieut. Walton, of the *Wells* cutter, giving an account of his proceedings consequent on Lord Dartmouth's letter of 18 Oct.—Admiralty Office.

The enclosures. The vessel Lieut. Walton was sent to watch at Amsterdam, after one attempt to sail, was finally unladen of her cargo and partly unrigged. Information was also obtained that if she attempted to go down the river she would certainly be searched at the Texel by the Dutch Admiralty.

AMERICAN EXPEDITION TO CANADA (1775).

Source.—*Calendar of Home Office Papers (1773-1775). Pp. 407-409.*

Home Office Papers

Hugh Finlay to ? Anthony Todd.

19 and 20 Sept.—The army under General Gage at Boston cannot be of much service there; it would require a very great force to penetrate any way into the country. Every American able to bear arms will take the field; they will avoid meeting the King's troops openly, will harass and pick them off from behind trees, hedges, or any cover, and will ever take possession of the ground left by the King's troops. The provincials, by handling arms, will become soldiers. They seem not to foresee the great misery that their non-importation and non-exportation will occasion among them. I am inclined to think that they entered into this association more with a design to cause troubles and commotions in England than from a conception that they can subsist for any time without our manufactures. The agreement not to export their produce will of itself bring them to implore Britain to permit them to send it out; thousands must starve else. As long as the King's troops act against the rebellious colonists, they will hang together, and be obedient to their leaders. If the troops shall be withdrawn, the people will have nothing to divert their attention from their situation; they will more forcibly feel the sad distress that non-exportation will inevitably spread in every province: every man will think for himself, they will become discontented, and will insist on making up the affair with the mother country. I am persuaded that after they are left to reflect coolly on their conduct they will return to their duty. They, no doubt, at present imagine that they will be supplied from Holland and France; indeed, it will hardly be possible wholly to hinder this; yet it will be as impossible for the Americans to get a twentieth part of what they'll want. A few ships of war can block up all their principal harbours, and a chain of small cruisers can do the rest. Necessity is the mother of invention. They will become expert in many manufactures, but without money in the country the manufacturer will find but little encouragement. Without foreign trade they'll have no money.

Every soldier on the continent would be well employed to drive the rebels from this province. The provincial troops have executed their plan so far. A body of them have gone round our works at St. John's, and have taken post on Sorrel River. By this means they cut off all communication with our little army by water, and they are now endeavouring to cut off the communication between St. John's and Montreal. If they succeed, our troops at St. John's can have no supply of provisions from any quarter, as the rebels are posted also at Isle aux Noix. We are not above 500 strong at Quebec. We lately had 900 Indian warriors in our interest; they have made their peace with the provincials, and are about returning to their homes. The rebels have nothing to fear from the Canadians; nine in ten are in their interests, and heartily wish them success. How have we been deceived in the Canadians! Many Englishmen in this province have taken infinite pains to set the Quebec Act in a most horrid light to the Canadians, and they have succeeded but too well. The Canadians look upon the rebels as their best friends. I shall not be surprised if many join them. We are in a bad situation in this place. The walls are in bad repair; in many places an enemy may easily enter the town. We have no cannon mounted. We have not a single armed vessel in our harbour. General Carleton, in whose military abilities we have great confidence, is at Montreal. Our Lieut.-Governor (Mr. Cramahé) and Col. McLean are doing everything in their power to put the town in a proper posture of defence. The British militia amount to 300, many of them well-wishers to the rebels. The Canadians muster about 600; few of them, I fear, willing to use their arms in defence of Quebec. I cannot suppose the provincials can bring artillery against this place. They know our strength, and I imagine they intend to take the town by assault. If they cannot effect it this fall, they will quarter themselves in the parishes round the town, and intercept all our supplies. If they cannot take us by assault nor starve us out, we hope to be reinforced from England very early in spring, for we can expect no assistance from the Canadian peasantry. Many of them have told me that they look on this rebellion only as a quarrel among Englishmen, in which they are no way immediately concerned, but that hereafter they'll reap great benefit if the colonists shall succeed in their plans. They have the notion that if the rebels get entire possession of the country, they'll be for ever exempted from paying taxes. If one asks them what will become of them when the British forces re-take the town in the spring, they answer that everything will be settled before that time; for that when the Ministry find Quebec in the hands of the Americans, they'll readily comply with every American demand. My opinion on the whole is this: Unless our troops at St. John's can join us here, the rebels will starve us; and even if they do, the flying parties of our enemies will intimidate the Canadians so much that no provisions will be brought to town. If the 500 at St. John's shall be able to join us, the rebels will not be able to enter the town unless hunger shall force us to abandon it. We are about 6,000 souls in Quebec. Perhaps the Canadians may return to their duty; in that case we have nothing to fear from the combined force of North America with such a General as our Governor at our head.

20 Sept.—There is advice from Montreal that the party on the Sorrel consists of 150 Canadians, headed by one Duggan, formerly a hairdresser of this place, and one James Livingstone, son of an Albany Dutchman, who resided long in Montreal. It is not known whether there are any provincials with them; it is supposed there are. It is imagined that it was this band of villains who fired on an artillery batteau loaded with stores for St. John's; they killed the men, 11 in number, and took her. Since the Governor's proclamation offering pardon to the Canadians of Duggan's party, many of them have deserted him, and they hourly expect to see Duggan and Livingstone brought dead or alive into Montreal. General Schuyler, commanding the expedition against this country, has commanded the parishes on the Sorrel or Richlieu River &c. to send 50 men from each, armed and properly provided, under pain of having fire and sword carried among them on refusal. I hope this mandate will open the eyes of the Canadians. The rebels could not have done us greater service.

Extract of a letter I received to-day from Montreal:—"The behaviour and appearance of our militia surpasses my most sanguine expectations, both as to numbers and conduct. Courage, loyalty, and cheerfulness are conspicuous in their countenances, and they do their duty cheerfully. I cannot help likewise expressing the pleasure I feel at the appearance of the peasantry returning to their duty."— Quebec.

RESOLUTIONS FAVOURING THE AMERI-CAN COLONIES (1775).

Source. — "Speech on Conciliation with America," *Edmund Burke.* Vol. i. of his Collected Works. London: G. Bell and Sons. 1909.

Burke

I wish, Sir, to repeal the Boston Port Bill, because (independently of the dangerous precedent of suspending the rights of the subject during the king's pleasure) it was passed, as I apprehend, with less regularity, and on more partial principles, than it ought. The corporation of Boston was not heard before it was condemned. Other towns, full as guilty as she was, have not had their ports blocked up. Even the restraining bill of the present session does not go to the length of the Boston Port Act. The same ideas of prudence, which induced you not to extend equal punishment to equal guilt, even when you were punishing, induced me, who mean not to chastise, but to reconcile, to be satisfied with the punishment already partially inflicted.

Ideas of prudence and accommodation to circumstances, prevent you from taking away the charters of Connecticut and Rhode Island, as you have taken away that of Massachusetts colony, though the crown has far less power in the two former provinces than it enjoyed in the latter; and though the abuses have been full as great, and as flagrant, in the exempted as in the punished. The same reasons of prudence and accommodation have weight with me in restoring the charter of Massachusetts Bay. Besides, Sir, the act which changes the charter of Massachusetts is in many particulars so exceptionable, that if I did not wish absolutely to repeal, I would by all means desire to alter it; as several of its provisions tend to the subversion of all public and private justice. Such, among others, is the power in the governor to change the sheriff at his pleasure; and to make a new returning officer for every special cause. It is shameful to behold such a regulation standing among English laws.

The act for bringing persons accused of committing murder under the orders of government to England for trial is but temporary. That act has calculated the probable duration of our quarrel with the colonies; and is accommodated to that supposed duration. I would hasten the happy moment of reconciliation; and therefore must, on my principle, get rid of that most justly obnoxious act.

The act of Henry the Eighth, for the trial of treasons, I do not mean to take away, but to confine it to its proper bounds and original intention; to make it expressly for trial of treasons (and the greatest treasons may be committed) in places where the jurisdiction of the crown does not extend.

Having guarded the privileges of local legislature, I would next secure to the colonies a fair and unbiassed judicature; for which purpose, Sir, I propose the following resolution: "That, from the time when the general assembly or general court of any colony or plantation in North America, shall have appointed by act of assembly, duly confirmed, a settled salary to the offices of the chief justice and other judges of the superior court, it may be proper that the said chief justice and other judges of the superior courts of such colony, shall hold his and their office and offices during their good behaviour; and shall not be removed therefrom, but when the said removal shall be adjudged by his Majesty in council, upon a hearing on complaint from the general assembly, or on a complaint from the governor, or council, or the house of representatives severally, or of the colony in which the said chief justice and other judges have exercised the said offices."

The next resolution relates to the courts of admiralty.

It is this:—"That it may be proper to regulate the courts of admiralty, or vice-admiralty, authorized by the fifteenth chapter of the fourth of George the Third, in such a manner as to make the same more commodious to those who sue, or are sued, in the said courts, and to provide for the more decent maintenance of the judges in the same."

These courts I do not wish to take away; they are in themselves proper establishments. This court is one of the capital securities of the act of navigation. The extent of its jurisdiction, indeed, has been increased; but this is altogether as proper, and is indeed on many accounts more eligible, where new powers were wanted, than a court absolutely new. But courts incommodiously situated, in effect, deny justice; and a court, partaking in the fruits of its own condemnation, is a robber. The congress complain, and complain justly, of this grievance.[7]

These are the three consequential propositions. I have thought of two or three more; but they come rather too near detail, and to the province of executive government; which I wish parliament always to superintend, never to assume. If the first six are granted, congruity will carry the latter three. If not, the things that remain unrepealed will be, I hope, rather unseemly encumbrances on the building, than very materially detrimental to its strength and stability.

---

[7] The Solicitor-General informed Mr. B. when the resolutions were separately moved, that the grievance of the judges partaking of the profits of the seizure had been redressed by office; accordingly the resolution was amended.

THE ARMIES UNDER HOWE AND CLINTON (1777).

Source. — *Gentleman's Magazine.* Vol. xlvii. (1777), pp. 573 *et seq.*

"Gentleman's Magazine"

An Historical Account of the Proceedings of the Armies under General Howe and Maj. Gen. Clinton, extracted from the Gazette Extraordinary, dated Tuesday, December 2.

These advices were brought by Maj. Cuyler, first aide-de-camp to General Sir William Howe, and are dated German Town, Oct. 10, 1777.

On the 30th of August the army under Gen. Howe landed on the West side of Elk river, and divided into two columns; one under the command of Lord Cornwallis, the other commanded by Lieut. Gen. Knyphausen.

On Sept. 3 (Major-General Grant, with six battalions, remaining at the head of Elk to preserve the communication with the fleet) the two columns joined on the road to Christien bridge. The Hessian and Anspach chasseurs defeated on their march a chosen corps of one thousand men from the enemy's army, with the loss of only 2 officers wounded, 3 men killed, and 19 wounded, when that of the enemy was not less than 50 killed, and many more wounded.

On the 6th Major-General Grant joined the army.

The whole marched on the 8th by Newark, and encamped that evening within four miles of the enemy, who moved early in the night, taking post on the heights on the eastern side of Brandywine creek.

On the 9th Lieut. Gen. Knyphausen marched with the left, as did Lord Cornwallis with the right, and both joined the next morning at Kennett's-square.

On the 11th the army advanced in two columns, that under Gen. Knyphausen to Chad's Ford, and arrived in front of the enemy about 10 o'clock; while the other column, under Lord Cornwallis &c., having marched 12 miles round to the forks of the Brandywine, crossed both branches, taking from thence the road to Dilworth in order to turn the enemy's right at Chad's Ford.

Gen. Washington, having intelligence of this movement, detached Gen. Sullivan to his right, with near 10,000 men, who took a strong position, with his left near to the Brandywine, both flanks being covered by very thick woods, and his artillery advantageously disposed.

About 4 o'clock the King's troops advanced, and Ld. Cornwallis having formed the line, the light infantry and chasseurs began the attack; the guards and grenadiers instantly advanced from the right, the whole under a heavy fire of artillery and musquetry: but they pushed on with an impetuosity not to be sustained by the enemy, who falling back into the woods in their rear, the King's troops entered with them, and pursued closely for near two miles.

After this success, a part of the enemy's right took a second position in a wood, from whence the 2d light infantry and chasseurs soon dislodged them; and from this time they did not rally again in force.

The 2d light infantry, 2d grenadiers and 4th brigade, moved forward a mile beyond Dilworth, where they attacked a corps of the enemy, strongly posted to cover the retreat of their army, which corps not being forced until after it was dark, the enemy's army escaped a total overthrow.

From the most correct accounts, the strength of the enemy's army was not less than 15,000 men, a part of which retired to Chester, and remained there that night; but the greater body did not stop until they reached Philadelphia. They had about 300 men killed, 600 wounded, and near 400 made prisoners.

The loss on the side of his Majesty's troops amounted to about 100 killed, and 488 wounded. Eight pieces of cannon, and a great quantity of military stores were taken from the enemy.

The army lay this night on the field of battle, and on the 12th Maj. Gen. Grant, with the first and second brigades, marched to Concord. Lord Cornwallis, with the light infantry and British grenadiers, joined him next day, and proceeded to Ash-Town within five miles of Chester.

On the same day Major M'Donell made Mr. McKinley, the new appointed President of the Lower Counties on Delaware, his prisoner.

Lieut. Col. Loos, with the combined battalion of Rhall's brigade, escorted the wounded and sick to Wilmington on the 14th.

On the 16th intelligence being received that the enemy were advancing on the Lancaster road, it was immediately determined to push forward and attack them; but a most violent fall of rain setting in, the intended attack became impracticable.

The enemy, apprised of the approach of the army, marched the whole night, and got to Yellow Springs, having, as is since known, all their small ammunition damaged by the rain. In their retreat they lost about 18 men killed, and some wounded.

On the 18th a detachment of light infantry was sent to the Valley Forge upon Schuylkill, where the enemy had a variety of stores, and a considerable magazine of flour, and were joined on the 20th by the guards.

Upon intelligence that Gen. Wayne was lying in the woods with a corps of 1,500 men, and four pieces of cannon, Maj. Gen. Grey was detached on the 20th to surprize him; and having, by the bayonet only, forced his pickets, he rushed in upon his encampment, killed and wounded not less than 300 on the spot, taking between 70 and 80 prisoners, including officers, their arms, and eight waggons loaded with baggage and stores. One captain of light infantry and three men were killed in the attack, and four men wounded. Gallantry in the troops, and good conduct in the General, were fully manifested upon this critical service.

On the 22d the army crossed the Schuylkill, at Fat Land Ford, without opposition; and on the 25th marched in two columns to German Town. Lord Cornwallis, with the British grenadiers, and two battalions of Hessian grenadiers, took possession of Philadelphia the next morning.

In the evening of the 26th, three batteries were begun, to act against the enemy's shipping that might approach the town. These batteries were unfinished when they were attacked by a number of gallies, gondolas, and other armed vessels; and the largest frigate, the *Delaware*, mounting 30 guns, anchored within 500 yards of the town. About ten in the morning they began a heavy cannonade; but the tide falling, the *Delaware* grounded, and was taken possession of by the marine company of grenadiers, commanded by Capt. Averne.

The smaller frigates and armed vessels were forced (except a schooner that was driven on shore) to return under the protection of a fort, where there were two floating batteries, with three range of sunken machines, to obstruct the passage of the river, the lowest row being three miles below the fort.

The enemy had a redoubt upon the Jersey shore at Billing's Point, with heavy guns in it, to prevent these machines from being weighed up, which 300 men posted there evacuated on the 1st of October; and Capt. Hammond immediately opened the navigation at that place, by removing a part of the chevaux de frize.

The enemy having received a reinforcement of 1,500 men from Peek's Kill, and 1,000 from Virginia, and presuming on the army being much weakened by the detachments to Philadelphia and Jersey, thought it a favourable time for them to risk an action. They accordingly marched at six in the evening of the 3d from their camp near Skippach-creek to German-Town, (about 16 miles,) where the bulk of the army was posted.

At three in the morning of the 4th the patrols discovered the enemy's approach, and the army was immediately ordered under arms.

About break of day the enemy began their attack; but the light infantry, being well supported, sustained the same with such determined bravery, that they could not make the least impression on them; and Major-Gen. Grant advancing with the right wing, the enemy's left gave way, and was pursued through a strong country between four and five miles: but such was the expedition with which they fled, that it was not possible to overtake them.

The enemy retired near twenty miles by several roads to Perkiomy-creek, and encamped upon Skippach-creek.

They saved all their cannon by withdrawing them early in the day.

By the best accounts, their loss was between two and three hundred killed, about 600 wounded, and upwards of 400 taken. Among the killed was Gen. Nash, with many other officers of all ranks, and 54 officers among the prisoners.

Since the battle of Brandywine 72 of their officers have been taken, exclusive of 10 belonging to the *Delaware* frigate.

On the 19th the army removed from German-Town to Philadelphia, as a more convenient situation for the reduction of Fort Island, which at present is an obstruction to the passage of the river, as the upper chevaux de frize cannot be removed until we have possession of that post; near which the enemy having intrenched about 800 men upon the Jersey shore, Col. Donop, with three battalions of Hessian grenadiers, the regiment of Mirback, and the infantry chasseurs, crossed the Delaware on the 21st instant, with directions to proceed to the attack of that post. Col. Donop led on the troops in the most gallant manner to the assault. They carried an extensive out-work, from whence the enemy were driven into an interior intrenchment, which could not be forced without ladders. The detachment, in moving up and returning from the attack, was much galled by the enemy's gallies and floating batteries.

Col. Donop and Lieut. Col. Minningerode being both wounded, the command devolved upon Lieut. Col. Linsing, who, after collecting all the wounded that could be brought off, returned with the detachment to camp.

There were several brave officers lost upon this occasion, in which the utmost ardour and courage were displayed by both officers and soldiers.

On the 23d, the *Augusta*, in coming up the river with some other ships of war, to engage the enemy's gallies near the fort, got aground, and, by some accident taking fire in the action, was unavoidably consumed. The *Merlin* sloop also grounded, and the other ships being obliged to remove to a distance from the explosion of the *Augusta*, it became expedient to evacuate and burn her also.

His Excellency concludes his letters with requesting additional cloathing for 5,000 Provincials, which, by including the new levies expected to be raised in that and the neighbouring countries, will certainly be wanting.

While these important services were transacting in Pennsylvania, Lieut. Gen. Clinton meditated an incursion into Jersey: his principal motive was to attempt a stroke against any detached corps of the enemy, if one offered; or, if not, to collect a considerable number of cattle, which would at the same time prove a seasonable refreshment to the troops, and deprive the enemy of resources which they much depended on.

The result of this expedition, after a little skirmishing with small parties of the enemy, was the collecting about 400 head of cattle, including 20 milch cows for the use of the hospital, 400 sheep, and a few horses, with the loss of about 40 men, killed, wounded, prisoners, and missing.

By a letter from Brig.-Gen. Campbell to Sir Henry Clinton, dated Staten Island, Aug. 23, it appears, that the enemy effected almost a total surprize of two battalions of the Jersey Provincials on that island; but that they had suffered severely for their temerity in making the descent, Col. Dongan having come up with their rear at the very instant when the rebels were using the greatest diligence in transporting their troops to the Jersey shore; and being joined by Brig.-Gen. Campbell with cannon, who took them in flank, about 150 surrendered themselves prisoners of war; and the remainder, of nearly the same number, retreating towards the extremity of the island, found means to cross over near Amboy.

Col. Buskirk's battalion being ordered to attack a party left to cover the enemy's boats, they did it with charge of bayonet, and obliged the party to retreat to the Jersey shore.

It further appears, that this descent was carried on by select and chosen troops, formed from three brigades, Sullivan's, Smallwood's, and De Bore's, and headed by their respective Generals, besides Drayton's and Ogden's battalions. There were taken in all 259 prisoners, among whom are 1 Lieut.-Colonel, 3 Majors, 2 Captains, and 15 inferior officers. Their loss in killed cannot be ascertained, but must have been considerable.[8]

In a letter from Lieut.-Gen. Sir Henry Clinton to Gen. Sir William Howe, dated Fort Montgomery, Oct. 9, an account is given of an attack upon Fort Clinton, Montgomery, &c. which reflects the greatest military honour on the conquerors.

The difficulties of the march over mountains, every natural obstruction, and all that art could invent to add to them, being surmounted, General Vaughan's corps was ordered to begin the attack on Fort Clinton, and dislodge, if possible, the enemy from their advanced station behind a stone breastwork, having in front, for half a mile, a most impenetrable abbatis. This the General, by his good disposition, obliged the enemy to quit, tho' supported by cannon, got possession of the wall, and there waited till Lieut.-Col. Campbell began his attack. The Colonel waited a favourable moment to attack Fort Clinton, which was a circular height, defended by a line for musquetry, with a barbet battery of three guns in the center, and flanked by two redoubts; the approaches to it thro' a continued abbatis of 400 yards, defensive every inch, and exposed to the fire of ten pieces of cannon. A brisk attack on the Montgomery side; the gallies with their oars approaching, firing, and even striking the fort; the men of war that moment appearing; the extreme ardour of the troops; in short, all determined the General to order the attack: Gen. Vaughan's spirited behaviour and good conduct did the rest. Having no time to lose, he particularly ordered that not a shot should be fired; in this he was strictly obeyed, and both redoubts &c. were stormed. Gen. Tryon advanced with one battalion to support Gen. Vaughan in case it might be necessary, and he arrived in time to join the cry of Victory!

A summons was sent to Fort Constitution; but the flag meeting with an insolent reception, unknown in any war, the General determined to chastise, and therefore an embarkation was ordered; but they found the fort evacuated in the greatest confusion, the storehouses burnt, but the cannon left unspiked.

Major-Gen. Tryon was detached to destroy the rebel settlement called the Continental Village, who burnt barracks for 1,500 men, several storehouses, and loaded waggons, this being the only establishment of the rebels in that part of the highlands, and the place from whence any neighbouring body of troops drew their supplies.

---

[8] The Provincial account of this action differs materially.

Sir James Wallace was ordered up the river at the same time, to find a passage through the chevaux de frize between Polypus Island and the Main, having under his protection a large detachment from the army, headed by Major Gen. Vaughan, from whose report, dated on board the *Friendship* off Esopus, Oct. 17, Gen. Howe takes occasion to applaud a very spirited piece of service performed by those two officers, who attacked the batteries, drove the rebels from their works, spiked and destroyed their guns; and Esopus "being a nursery for almost every villain in the country," the General landed and reduced every house to ashes, while Sir James Wallace burnt their shipping and small craft.

Return of Cannon, Stores, Ammunition, etc., taken and destroyed on this Expedition.

Cannon 67, from six to two pounders. Two frigates built for 30 and 36 guns were burnt by the rebels on the forts being taken. The guns aboard them, and two gallies, which were likewise burnt, amounted to above 30. One sloop with 10 guns fell into our hands. The whole loss above 100 pieces.

Powder, cartridges fitted, cannon and musquet shot, immense quantities.

Every article belonging to the laboratory in the greatest perfection. Other stores, such as portfires, match, harness, spare gun-carriages, tools, instruments, &c. &c. in great plenty. A large quantity of provisions. The boom and chain which ran across the river from Fort Montgomery to St. Anthony's Nose is supposed to have cost 70,000*l.* Another boom which was destroyed near Fort Constitution must likewise have cost the rebels much money and labour. Barracks for 1,500 men were destroyed by Major-Gen. Tryon at Continental Village, besides several storehouses and loaded waggons, of the articles contained in which no accounts could be taken.

CHATHAM'S LAST LETTER AND SPEECH (1778).

Source.—*Correspondence of William Pitt, Earl of Chatham.* Vol. iv., pp. 518 *et seq.*

Correspondence of Chatham and "London Magazine"

[From a draught in the handwriting of Lord Pitt.]

The Earl of Chatham to the Duke of Richmond, April 6, 1778.

Lord Chatham presents his respects to the Duke of Richmond, and desires to express his best thanks for the great honour of the communication of the motion intended by his Grace on Tuesday.

It is an unspeakable concern to him, to find himself under so very wide a difference with the Duke of Richmond, as between the *sovereignty* and *allegiance* of America, that he despairs of bringing about successfully any honourable issue. He is inclined to try it, before *this bad* grows worse. Some weakness still continues in his hands; but he hopes to be in town to-morrow.[9]

[Report of the Earl of Chatham's Last Speech, from the "London Magazine."]

The Earl of Chatham followed Lord Weymouth.—

He appeared to be extremely feeble, and spoke with that difficulty of utterance which is the characteristic of severe indisposition. His Lordship began with declaring that his ill health had for some time obliged him to absent himself from the performance of his parliamentary duty; he rejoiced, however, that he was yet alive to give his vote against so impolitic, so inglorious a measure as the acknowledgment of the independency of America; and declared he would much rather be in his grave than see the lustre of the British throne tarnished, the dignity of the empire disgraced, the glory of the nation sunk to such a degree as it must be, when the dependency of America on the sovereignty of Great Britain was given up. The Earl next adverted to the conduct of the court of France, and observed, that at a crisis like the present, he would openly speak his sentiments, although they might turn out to be dangerous. As a reason for throwing off reserve, he said he did not approve of halting between two opinions, when there was no middle path; that it was necessary absolutely to declare either for peace or war, and when

[9] On the "morrow" Lord Chatham appeared in the House of Lords *for the last time.*

the former could not be preserved with honour, the latter ought to be declared without hesitation. Having made this remark, he asked, where was the ancient spirit of the nation, that a foreign power was suffered to bargain for that commerce which was her natural right, and enter into a treaty with her own subjects, without instantly resenting it? Could it be possible that we were the same people who but fifteen years ago were the envy and admiration of all the world? How were we altered! and what had made the alteration? He feared there was something in the dark, something lurking near the throne, which gave motion to administration—something unseen, which caused such pusillanimous, such timid, such dastardly councils. What! were we to sit down in an ignominious tameness? to say, "Take from us what you will, but in God's name let us be at peace?" Were we blinded by despair? Could we forget that we were Englishmen? Could we forget that the nation had stood the Danish irruptions? had stood the irruptions of other nations! had stood the inroads of the Scotch! had stood the Norman conquests! had stood the threatened invasion by the famous Spanish armada, and the various efforts of the Bourbon compacts! Why, then, should we now give up all, without endeavouring to prevent our losses, without a blow, without an attempt to resent the insults offered us? If France and Spain were for war, why not try an issue with them? If we fell afterwards, we should fall decently, and like men.

Having spoken with some enthusiasm upon these points, his Lordship said he waged war against no set of men, neither did he wish for any of their employments: he then reverted to the subject of American independency; and after recalling the attention of their lordships to the extent and revenue of the estate of the crown of England, when the present King came into the possession of it, asked what right the Houses of Parliament had to deprive the Prince of Wales, the Bishop of Osnaburgh, and the other rising hopes of the beloved royal family, of the inheritance of the thirteen American provinces? Sooner than consent to take away from any of the heirs of the Princess Sophia what they had a legal and natural right to expect to possess, he declared he would see the Prince of Wales, the Bishop of Osnaburgh, and the rest of the young princes, brought down to the committee, and hear them consent to lose their inheritance. The Earl declared he was exceedingly ill; but as long as he could crawl down to that House, and had strength to raise himself on his crutches, or to lift his hand, he would vote against the giving up the dependency of America on the sovereignty of Great Britain; and if no other lord was of opinion with him, he would singly protest against the measure.

With regard to our power to carry on the war, or commence a new one with France, there were, he said, means, though he knew not what; if, however, he was called upon to give his advice, he would give it honestly; and though, from his exceeding ill state of health, he feared he had not abilities to insure to the execution of his measures the wished-for success, he would make some amends by his sincerity.

KING GEORGE'S MESSAGE AND THE SPAN-ISH MANIFESTO (1779).

Source.—*Gentleman's Magazine.* Vol. xlix., pp. 324 *et seq.*

"Gentleman's Magazine"

Ld. Weymouth, principal secretary of state for the southern departments, presented the following message from his Majesty to the H. of Lords. At the same time Ld. North laid the same message before the H. of C.

COPY OF THE KING'S MESSAGE.
"George R.

"The ambassador of the King of Spain having delivered a paper to Lord Viscount Weymouth, and signified that he has received orders from his court immediately to withdraw from this country; his Majesty has judged it necessary to direct a copy of that paper to be laid before the House of Commons as a matter of the highest importance to the crown and people; and his Majesty acquaints them, at the same time, that he has found himself obliged, in consequence of this hostile declaration, to recal his ambassador from Madrid.

"His Majesty declares, in the most solemn manner, that his desire to preserve and to cultivate peace and friendly intercourse with the court of Spain has been uniform and sincere; and that his conduct towards that power has been guided by no other motives or principles than those of good faith, honour, and justice; and his Majesty sees with the greatest surprize the pretences on which this declaration is grounded, as some of the grievances enumerated in that paper have *never* come to the knowledge of his Majesty, either by representation on the part of the Catholic King, or by intelligence from any other quarter; and in all those cases where applications have been received, the matter of complaint has been treated with the *utmost attention*, and put into a course of *enquiry* and *redress.*

"His Majesty has the firmest confidence that his faithful Commons will, with that zeal and public spirit which he has so often experienced, support his Majesty in his resolution to exert all the power and the resources of the Nation, to resist and repel any hostile attempts of the court of Spain; and that, by the blessing of God on the rectitude of his intentions, and the equity of his cause, his Majesty will be able to withstand and defeat the *unjust* and *dangerous* enterprizes of his enemies, against the honour of his crown, and the Commerce, the Rights, and the common interests, of all his subjects."

The manifesto above alluded to, which the Spanish ambassador presented to Ld. Weymouth, was as follows:

COPY OF THE SPANISH MANIFESTO.

"All the world has been witness to the noble impartiality of the King in the midst of the disputes of the court of London with its American Colonies and with France. Besides which his Majesty, having learned that his powerful mediation was desired, generously made an offer of it, which was accepted by the Belligerent Powers, and for this motive only a ship of war was sent on the part of his Britannic Majesty to one of the ports of Spain. The King has taken the most energetic steps, and such as ought to have produced the most happy effect, to bring those powers to an accommodation equally honourable to both parties; proposing for this end wise expedients for smoothing difficulties, and preventing the calamities of war. But although his Majesty's propositions, and particularly those of his *ultimatum*, have been conformable to those which at other times the court of London itself had appeared to judge proper for an accommodation, and which were also quite as moderate, they have been rejected in a manner that fully proves the little desire which the British cabinet has to restore peace to Europe, and to preserve the King's Friendship. In effect, the conduct of that cabinet, with regard to his Majesty, during the whole course of the negociation, has had for its object, to prolong it for more than eight months, either by vain pretences, or by answers which could not be more inconclusive; whilst, in this interval, the insults on the Spanish flag, and the violation of the King's Territories, were carried on to an incredible excess; prizes have been made, ships have been searched and plundered, and a great number of them have been fired upon, which have been obliged to defend themselves; the registers have been opened and torn in pieces, and even the packets of the court found on board the King's packet boats.

"The dominions of the crown in America have been threatened, and they have gone to the dreadful extremity of raising the Indian nations called the Chatcas, Cheroquies, and Chicachas, against the innocent inhabitants of Louisiana, who would have been the victims of the rage of these barbarians, if the Chatcas themselves had not repented and revealed all that the seduction of the English had planned. The sovereignty of his Majesty in the province of Darien, and on the coast of St. Blas, has been usurped; the governor of Jamaica having granted to a rebel Indian the commission of Captain-General of those Provinces.

"In short the territory of the Bay of Honduras has been recently violated by exercising acts of hostility, and other excesses against the Spaniards, who have been imprisoned and whose houses have been invaded; besides which, the court of London has hitherto neglected to accomplish what the 16th article of the last Treaty of Paris stipulated relative to that Coast.

"Grievances so numerous, so weighty, and recent, have been at different times the object of complaints made in the King's name, and stated in memorials which were delivered either to the British ministers at London, or transmitted to them through the channel of the English ambassador at Madrid; but although the answers which were received have been friendly, his Majesty has hitherto obtained no other satisfaction than to see the insults repeated, which lately have amounted to the number of one hundred.

"The King, proceeding with the sincerity and candour which characterize him, has formally declared to the court of London, from the commencement of its disputes with France, that the court of England should be the rule of that which Spain would hold.

"His Majesty likewise declared to that court, that at the time their differences with that of Paris might be accommodated, it would be absolutely necessary to regulate those which had arisen, or might still arise, with Spain; and with the plan of mediation which was sent to the underwritten ambassador the 28th of last September, and which was by him delivered to the British ministry in the beginning of October, a plan of which Lord Grantham was apprized, and of which he received a copy, his Majesty declared in positive terms to the Belligerent Powers, that in consideration of the insults which his subjects and dominions had suffered, and likewise of the attempts levelled against his rights, he should be under the necessity of taking his part, in case the negociation, instead of being continued with sincerity, should be broken off, or should produce no effect.

"The causes of complaint given by the court of London not having ceased, and that court shewing no disposition to give reparation for them, the King has resolved, and orders his ambassador to declare, that the honour of his crown, the protection which he owes to his subjects, and his own personal dignity, do not permit him to suffer their insults to continue, and to neglect any longer the reparation of those already received; and that in this view, notwithstanding the pacific disposition of his Majesty, and even the particular inclination he has always had and expressed for cultivating the friendship of his Britannick Majesty, he finds himself under the disagreeable necessity of making use of all the means which the Almighty has intrusted him with to obtain that justice which he has solicited by so many ways without being able to acquire: in confiding on the justice of his cause, his Majesty hopes that the consequences of this resolution will not be imputed to him before God or man; and that other nations will form a suitable idea of this resolution, by comparing it to the conduct which they themselves have experienced on the part of the British ministry.

"Signed LE MARQUIS D'ALMODOVAR.

"LONDON, *16 June, 1779.*"

These important papers being read, Lord Weymouth moved, That an humble address be presented to his Majesty (and Lord North moved the same in the House of Commons), to assure his Majesty of support, &c. This event, though not unexpected, occasioned warm debates in both houses. All were for agreeing to the address; but the Lords and gentlemen in opposition were for adding a condition, "provided his Majesty would discard from his councils the present ministry." After much altercation, and many severe charges of maladministration, the condition was rejected, and the addresses, as originally moved, passed by a great majority in both houses.

SOCIETY AT BRIGHTHELMSTON (BRIGH-TON) IN 1779.

Source.—Diarists quoted in *History of Brighthelmston*. John Ackerson Erredge. Brighton, 1862.

J. A. Erredge

(A.) THE LIBRARIES.

There is a sort of rivalry between the two Librarians on the Steyne, as to their subscription books; which shall most justly deserve the title of the book of Numbers.—There is a constant struggle between them, which shall be most courteous; and the effects are those usually consequent upon an opposition. Sir Christopher Caustic, this morning was turning over the leaves, at Bowen's, which contain the names of the subscribers. Mr. Bowen bowed *a la Novarre* or *Gallini*, and with offered pen and ink, craved the honour of—an additional name: this being his first season, and having been purposely misinformed by some would-be-witty wag; "Sir," said Mr. Bowen, displaying, all the time, two irregular rows of remarkably white teeth, "yours will stand immediately after that of the Honourable Charles James Fox, Esq., and before that of Mrs. Franco, the rich Jew's lady. Esquire W——d's was to have been on the medium line, but, poor gentleman, he is unfortunately *detained* near London, on *emergent* business." To what a degree was the dealer in stationery let down, when he was afterwards regularly rectified; when by explanatory notes, and critical commentations, he came to be fully informed that the individual Mr. Fox in question was not the celebrated senator of that name, but an Irish *Jontleman*, who condescends in winter to keep a chop house at the corner of the play-house passage, in Bow Street, Covent Garden; and every autumnal season, has frequent opportunities of storming and swearing at the ladies who may have the good fortune to belong to the Brighthelmstone company of Comedians, he being sole manager thereof. And such management!—*Scarrons Rancour*, who filled all the characters in a play by himself, was a fool to him....

Mr. Thomas, the other librarian, must be noticed in turn. He hath been years enough practising small talk with the ladies and gentlemen upon the Steyne, and hath arrived at a surprising degree of precision in pronouncing French-English. He is now reading the newspaper to some of his subscribers, with an audible voice, and repeatedly calls a detached body of troops a *corpse*; a *tour* he improves into a *tower*; and delivers his words in a *promiscas* manner. It is near seven in the evening, and the widow Fussic has just waddled into his shop, with a parasol in her right, and a spying-glass in her left hand. Thomas offers her a *General Adver-tiser*. "Lord bless me!" says she, "Mr. Thomas, how damp this paper is, tho' it has come so far, and must have been printed so long since! What reason can you give for it?"—Mr. Thomas observes, considers and explains, in a most explicit man-ner, the cause and the effect, to the inquisitive lady, naturally speaking, as a body may say; proving to a demonstration, according to Candide, that there can be no effect without a cause; and that of course, damp papers, closely compressed, will continue damp a considerable time. In the interim, Miss Fanny Fussic stares and whispers to her brother Bobby, while he is subscribing to a raffle, that Mr. Thomas must be a most prodigious man monstrously intelligent, and withal, that he is amazingly communicative: "He knows but every-thing," says she, "and tells but every-thing he knows."

(B.) The Raffles.

Every article of convenience, every trinket of luxury, is transferred by this uncertain, quick mode of conveyance. Not a shop without its rattle-trap,—rat-tle, rattle, rattle, morning and evening. Here may be seen,—walk in and see,—an abridgement of the wisdom of this world;—the pomps and vanities are at large, varying like yonder evanescent clouds. Observe the fond parent initiating her for-ward offspring in the use of the dice-box, and herself setting the example; yet may she wonder, at some future day, and think her throw in life's raffle extremely severe, that a propensity to that and similar habits should continue and increase.

THE GORDON NO-POPERY RIOTS (1780).

Source.—*Letters of Horace Walpole.*

Horace Walpole

To Rev. William Cole, Strawberry Hill, June 15, 1780.

You may like to know one is alive, dear sir, after a massacre and the conflagration of a capital. I was in it, both on the Friday, and on the Black Wednesday; the most horrible sight I ever beheld, and which, for six hours together, I expected to end in half the town being reduced to ashes. I can give you little account of the original of this shocking affair; negligence was certainly its nurse, and religion only its godmother. The ostensible author is in the Tower. Twelve or fourteen thousand men have quelled all tumults; and as no bad account is come from the country, except for a moment at Bath, and as eight days have passed—nay, more, since the commencement—I flatter myself the whole nation is shocked at the scene; and that, if plan there was, it was laid only in and for the metropolis. The lowest and most villainous people, and to no great amount, were almost the sole actors.

I hope your electioneering riotry has not, nor will mix in these tumults. It would be most absurd; for lord Rockingham, the duke of Richmond, Sir George Saville, and Mr. Burke, the patrons of toleration, were devoted to destruction as much as the ministers. The rails torn from Sir George's house were the chief weapons and instruments of the mob. For the honour of the nation I should be glad to have it proved that the French were the engineers. You and I have lived too long for comfort—shall we close our eyes in peace? I will not trouble you more about the arms I sent you: I should like that they were those of the family of Boleyn; and since I cannot be sure they were not, why should not I fancy them so? I revert to the prayer for peace. You and I, that can amuse ourselves with our books and papers, feel as much indignation at the turbulent as they have scorn for us. It is hard at least that they who disturb nobody can have no asylum in which to pursue their innoxious indolence! Who is secure against Jack Straw and a whirlwind? How I abominate Mr. Banks and Dr. Solander, who routed the poor Otaheitans out of the centre of the ocean, and carried our abominable passions amongst them! not even that poor little speck could escape European restlessness. Well, I have seen many tempestuous scenes, and outlived them! the present prospect is too thick to see through—it is well hope never forsakes us. Adieu!

Yours most sincerely.

SURRENDER OF CORNWALLIS (1781).

Source.—*Gentleman's Magazine.* Vol. li., p. 539.

"Gentleman's Magazine"

Whitehall.—By Sir H. Clinton's letter to Lord G. Germaine, dated off Chesapeak, October 29, and brought by the *Rattlesnake* sloop, capt. Melcombe, it appears that "the fleet and army, which sailed from the Hook on the 19th, arrived off Cape Charles on the 24th, when they had the mortification to hear that lord Cornwallis had proposed terms of capitulation to the enemy on the 18th. This intelligence was brought by the pilot of the *Charon*, and some other persons who came off from the shore, and said they had made their escape from York on the 18th, and had not heard any firing there since the day before. The *Nymph* frigate also arriving from New-York, says the General, brought me a letter from his lordship, dated the 15th, the desponding tenor of which gives me the most alarming apprehensions of its truth.

Since then we have been plying off the Capes, with variable and hard gales of wind, to the present hour, without being able to procure any further information, except from two men taken in a Canoe, whose report exactly corresponds with the former.

Comparing, therefore, the intelligence given by those people, and several others since come in, with the purport of lord Cornwallis's letter, a copy of which I have the honour to inclose for your lordship's information; we cannot entertain the least doubt of his lordship's having capitulated, and that we are unfortunately too late to relieve him; which being the only object of the expedition, the admiral has determined upon returning with his fleet to Sandy Hook.

I beg leave to mention to your lordship, that the army is under the greatest obligations to the admirals, the captains, and the officers of the king's ships, for the cheerfulness with which they submitted to many and great inconveniences for our accommodation on this service."

The Dispatches from admiral Graves were to the same effect as the above from Sir H. Clinton.

The terms of capitulation have not yet officially been received.

PRELIMINARIES OF EUROPEAN PEACE (1783).

Source.—*Gentleman's Magazine.* Vol. liii., p. 91.

"Gentleman's Magazine"

SUBSTANCE OF THE PRELIMINARY ARTICLES OF PEACE BETWEEN GREAT BRITAIN AND FRANCE, SPAIN, AND THE UNITED STATES OF AMERICA.

Between Great Britain and France.

Peace to take place in all parts of the world as soon as the preliminaries are ratified. Newfoundland to remain to England as before the war; and, to prevent disputes about boundaries, the French fishery shall commence from Cape St. John on the eastern side, and, going round by the north, shall have for its boundary Cape Ray on the western side.

The islands of St. Pierre and Miquelon to be ceded to the French, with liberty to fish in the Gulph of St. Laurence.

The French to have St. Lucia and Tobago.

The English to have Granada and the Grenadines, St. Vincent's, Dominica, St. Kitt's, Nevis, and Montserrat; the subjects of the French King that choose to leave these islands, to be allowed 18 months to settle their affairs and dispose of their effects.

In Africa, the river Senegal and its forts to be ceded to France, and the island of Goree to be restored.

Fort St. James and Gambia to remain to England. The gum trade to remain as before the war.

All the establishments formerly belonging to the French in India, to be put on the same footing as before the war, and the freedom of trade on the coasts of Orixa, Coromandel, and Malabar, to be free to the French either as private traders, or as a company.

Pondicherry, Kerical to be restored to the French with the districts of Valanour and Bahour, and the four contiguous Magans, Mahé, and the Comptoir at Surat, to the French.

The allies of France and England in India, to be invited to accede to the present pacification, and four months allowed them to make their decision. In case of refusal no assistance to be given the allies on either side.

Great Britain renounces every claim whatsoever relative to Dunkirk.

Commissioners to be appointed to agree upon new arrangements of trade on the footing of reciprocity and mutual convenience.

All conquests on either side not included in those articles to be restored.

The rest of the treaty between France and England respects the time when the cessions are to be made, the prisoners released, the captures to cease, and the treaty ratified, which is fixed for one month or sooner, if it may be.

Between Great Britain and Spain.

Minorca to be ceded to Spain, and East and West Florida.

The English to have liberty to cut and carry away logwood, in a district that shall be allotted them.

Spain to restore to Great Britain the islands of Providence, and the Bahamas without exception.

All other conquests of what kind soever to be mutually restored; and all other treaties not herein mentioned to be in full force as heretofore.

The other part of the treaty exactly the same with France.

Between Great Britain and the United States of America.

His Britannic Majesty acknowledges the United States to be free, sovereign, and independent States, treats with them as such, and relinquishes all claim whatever to the lands and territories included within certain boundaries, which boundaries shall be described and delineated in a future Magazine.

The people of the United States shall continue to enjoy their fishery, in as ample a manner, as heretofore, on the coasts wherever British fishermen use; but not to dry their fish where settlements are actually made, or may hereafter be made, without previous agreement.

That creditors on either side shall meet with no lawful impediments, to recover their debts heretofore contracted.

That Congress shall earnestly recommend to their respective legislatures, to provide for the restitution of all estates, rights and properties belonging to real British subjects, or such as were resident in districts in the possession of his Majesty's arms, and who have not borne arms against the United States. And that persons of any other description shall have free liberty to remain in any part of any of the Thirteen United States for the term of twelve months unmolested in their endeavours for the recovery of their estates, &c. And that Congress shall recommend to the several States a revision of all acts regarding the premises, and to render the said laws consistent, not only with justice and equity, but with that spirit of reconciliation which, on the return of the blessings of peace, should universally prevail; so that the estates of persons of the above description may have their said estates restored, they refunding for the same the bona fide purchase money to the present possessors; nor shall persons having any interest in such confiscated lands, either by debts, marriage settlements, or otherwise, meet with any lawful impediment in the prosecution for the same.

That there shall be no farther confiscations made, nor prosecutions commenced against any persons for or on account of the part they may have taken in the present war.

That there shall be a perpetual peace between the contracting parties, and all hostilities both by sea and land shall forthwith cease; that the troops of his Britannic Majesty shall be immediately withdrawn, and that all American artillery shall remain in the forts and places that shall be evacuated.

The navigation of the Mississippi, from its source to the Ocean, to be free to the subjects of both States.

A VIOLENT ELECTION CONTEST (1784).

Source.—*Cowper's Letters*. Thomas Wright. London: Hodder and Stoughton. 1904. Vol. ii., pp. 194-197.

Cowper's "Letters"

To Rev. John Newton, April 26, 1784.

... The candidates for this county have set an example of economy, which other candidates would do well to follow having come to an agreement on both sides to defray the expenses of their voters, but to open no houses for the entertainment of the rabble; a reform, however, which the rabble did not at all approve of, and testified their dislike of it by a riot. A stage was built, from which the orators had designed to harangue the electors. This became the first victim of their fury. Having very little curiosity to hear what gentlemen could say who would give them nothing better than words, they broke it in pieces, and threw the fragments upon the hustings. The sheriff, the members, the lawyers, the voters, were instantly put to flight. They rallied, but were again routed by a second assault, like the former. They then proceeded to break the windows of the inn to which they had fled; and a fear prevailing that at night they would fire the town, a proposal was made by the freeholders to face about and endeavour to secure them. At that instant a rioter, dressed in a merry-andrew's jacket, stepped forward, and challenged the best man among them. Olney sent the hero to the field, who made him repent of his presumption. Mr. Ashburner was he. Seizing him by the throat, he shook him,—he threw him to the earth, he made the hollowness of his skull resound by the application of his fists, and dragged him into custody without the least damage to his person. Animated by this example, the other freeholders followed it: and in five minutes twenty-eight out of thirty ragamuffins were safely lodged in gaol....

THE COUNTRY POST (1785).

Source.—William Cowper, *The Task.* Book iv.

Cowper's "Task"

Hark! 'tis the twanging horn! O'er yonder bridge,
That with its wearisome but needful length
Bestrides the wintry flood, in which the moon
Sees her unwrinkled face reflected bright,
He comes, the herald of a noisy world,
With spattered boots, strapped waist, and frozen locks,
News from all nations lumbering at his back.
True to his charge, the close-packed load behind,
Yet careless what he brings, his one concern
Is to conduct it to the destined inn,
And having dropped the expected bag—pass on.
He whistles as he goes, light-hearted wretch,
Cold and yet cheerful: messenger of grief
Perhaps to thousands, and of joy to some,
To him indifferent whether grief or joy.
Houses in ashes, and the fall of stocks,
Births, deaths, and marriages, epistles wet
With tears that trickled down the writer's cheeks
Fast as the periods from his fluent quill,
Or charged with amorous sighs of absent swains,
Or nymphs responsive, equally affect
His horse and him, unconscious of them all.
But oh the important budget! ushered in
With such heart-shaking music, who can say
What are its tidings? have our troops awaked?
Or do they still, as if with opium drugged,
Snore to the murmurs of the Atlantic wave?
Is India free? and does she wear her plumed
And jewelled turban with a smile of peace,
Or do we grind her still? The grand debate,
The popular harangue, the tart reply,
The logic, and the wisdom, and the wit,
And the loud laugh—I long to know them all;
I burn to set the imprisoned wranglers free,

And give them voice and utterance once again.

HIS MAJESTY'S SPEECH (1787).

Source.—*Annual Register*. Vol. xxix., pp. 268 *et seq.* of *State Papers*.

"Annual Register"

His Majesty's most gracious Speech to both Houses of Parliament, on the opening of the fourth Session of the sixteenth Parliament of Great Britain, on Tuesday the 23d of January, 1787.

My Lords and Gentlemen,

"I have particular satisfaction in acquainting you, that since I last met you in parliament, the tranquillity of Europe has remained uninterrupted, and that all foreign powers continue to express their friendly disposition to this country.

"I have concluded a treaty of navigation and commerce with the Most Christian king, a copy of which shall be laid before you. I must recommend it to you to take such measures as you shall judge proper for carrying it into effect; and I trust you will find that the provisions contained in it are calculated for the encouragement of industry and the extension of lawful commerce in both countries, and by promoting a beneficial intercourse between our respective subjects, appear likely to give additional permanence to the blessings of peace. I shall keep the same salutary objects in view in the commercial arrangements which I am negociating with other powers.

"I have also given directions for laying before you a copy of a convention agreed upon between me and the Catholic king, for carrying into effect the sixth article of the last treaty of peace.

Gentlemen of the House of Commons,

"I have ordered the estimates for the present year to be laid before you; and I have the fullest reliance on your readiness to make due provision for the several branches of the public service.

"The state of the revenue will, I am persuaded, continue to engage your constant attention, as being essentially connected with the national credit, and the prosperity and safety of my dominions.

My Lords and Gentlemen,

"A plan has been formed, by my direction, for transporting a number of convicts, in order to remove the inconvenience which arose from the crowded state of the gaols in different parts of the kingdom; and you will, I doubt not, take such further measures as may be necessary for this purpose.

"I trust you will be able this session to carry into effect regulations for the ease of the merchants, and for simplifying the public accounts in the various branches of the revenue; and rely upon the uniform continuance of your exertions in pursuit of such objects as may tend still further to improve the national resources, and to promote and confirm the welfare and happiness of my people."

CHARACTERISTICS OF THE EAST INDIA COMPANY (1788).

Source. — *Speech in the Impeachment of Warren Hastings, Esq.*
Edmund Burke. Vol. vii. of his Collected Works. London: G. Bell
and Sons. 1911.

Burke

I must however remark, before I go further, that there is something in the representation of the East-India Company, in their oriental territory, different from that, perhaps, of any other nation that has ever transported any part of its power from one country to another. The East-India Company, in India, is not properly a branch of the British nation, it is only a deputation of individuals. When the Tartars entered into China, when the Arabs and Tartars successively entered into Hindostan, when the Goths and Vandals penetrated into Europe, when the Normans forced their way into England, indeed in all conquests, migrations, settlements, and colonizations, the new people came as the offset of a nation. The Company in India does not exist as a national colony. In effect and substance, nobody can go thither that does not go in its service. The English in India are nothing but a seminary for the succession of officers. They are a nation of placemen; — they are a commonwealth without a people; they are a state made up wholly of magistrates. There is nothing to be in propriety called people, to watch, to inspect, to balance against the power of office. The power of office, so far as the English nation is concerned, is the sole power in the country. The consequence of which is, that being a kingdom of magistrates, what is commonly called the *esprit du corps* is strong in it. This spirit of the body predominates equally in all parts; by which the members must consider themselves as having a common interest, and that common interest separated both from that of the country which sent them out, and from that of the country in which they act. No control upon them exists; none, I mean, in persons who understand their language, who understood their manners, or can apply their conduct to the laws. Therefore, in a body so constituted confederacy is easy, and has been general. Your lordships are not to expect that that should happen in such a body which never happened in any body or corporation, that is, that they should in any instance be a proper check and control upon themselves. It is not in the nature of things. The fundamental principle of the whole of the East-India Company's system is monopoly in some sense or other. The same principle predominates in the service abroad and the service at home; and both systems are united into one, animated with the same spirit, that is, with the corporate spirit. The whole, taken together, is such as has not been seen in the examples of the Moors, the Portuguese, the Spaniards, the Romans; in no old, in no recent examples. The Dutch may resemble it, but they have not an empire properly so denominated. By means of this peculiar circumstance it has not been difficult for Mr. Hastings to embody abuse, and to put himself at the head of a regular system of corruption.

Another circumstance in that service is deserving of notice. Except in the highest parts of all, the emoluments of office do not in any degree correspond with the trust, nor the nature of the office with its name. In other official systems the style, in general, is above the function; here is it the reverse. Under the name of junior merchant, senior merchant, writer, and other petty appellations of the counting-house, you have magistrates of high dignity, you have administrators of revenues truly royal;—you have judges civil, and in some respects criminal, who pass judgment upon the greatest properties of a great country. The legal public emoluments that belong to them are very often so inadequate to the real dignity of the character, that it is impossible, almost absolutely impossible, for the subordinate parts of it, which though subordinate are stations of power, to exist as Englishmen who look at a fortune to be enjoyed at home as their ultimate object, and to exist in a state of perfect incorruption in that service.

In some parts of Europe it is true that the greatest situations are often attended with but little emolument; yet still they are filled. Why? Because reputation, glory, fame, the esteem, the love, the tears of joy which flow from happy sensibility, the honest applauses of a grateful country, sometimes pay the cares, anxieties, and toils which wait on great situations in the commonwealth: and in these, they pay in money what cannot be paid in fame and reputation. It is the reverse in the service of the India Company. Glory is not the lot of subordinated merit; and all the subordinate parts of the gradation are officers who, in comparison with the offices and duties intrusted with them, are miserably provided for; whereas the chief of each great presidency has emoluments securing him against every mode of temptation. But if this has not secured the head, we may easily judge how the members are to be coerced. Mr. Hastings at the head of the service, with high legal emoluments, has fouled his hands and sullied his government with bribes. He has substituted oppression and tyranny in the place of legal government. With all that unbounded, licentious power which he has assumed over the public revenues, instead of endeavouring to find a series of gradual, progressive, honourable, and adequate rewards for the persons who serve the public in the subordinate but powerful situations, he has left them to prey upon the people without the smallest degree of control. In default of honest emolument, there is the unbounded license of power; and (as one of the honestest and ablest servants of the Company said to me in conversation) the civil service of the Company resembled the military service of the Mahrattas—little pay, but unbounded license to plunder. I do not say that some of the salaries given in India would not sound well here; but when you consider the nature of the trusts, the dignity of the situation, whatever the name of them may be, the powers that are granted, the hopes that every man has of establishing himself at home,—I repeat, it is a source of infinite grievance—of infinite abuse: of which source of corrupt power we charge Mr. Hastings with having availed himself in filling up the void of direct pay, by finding out and countenancing every kind of oblique and unjust emolument; though it must be confessed that he is far from being solely guilty of this offence.

Another circumstance which distinguishes the East-India Company is the youth of the persons who are employed in the system of that service. The servants have almost universally been sent out to begin their progress and career in active occupation, and in the exercise of high authority, at that period of life which in all other places has been employed in the course of a rigid education. To put the matter in a few words, they are transferred from slippery youth to perilous independence, from perilous independence to inordinate expectations, from inordinate expectations to boundless power. School-boys without tutors, minors without guardians, the world is let loose upon them, with all its temptations; and they are let loose upon the world, with all the powers that despotism involves.

CORN IMPORTS AND EXPORTS (1789).

Source.—*Annual Register, 1789, pp. 279 et seq.*

"Annual Register"

AN ACCOUNT OF THE QUANTITIES OF ALL CORN AND GRAIN EXPORTED FROM, AND IMPORTED INTO, ENGLAND AND SCOTLAND, WITH THE BOUNTIES AND DRAWBACKS PAID, AND THE DUTIES RECEIVED, THEREON, FOR ONE YEAR, ENDED THE 5TH OF JANUARY, 1790.

EXPORTED.

	British (Quarters).	Foreign (Quarters).	Bounties and Drawbacks paid.		
England, 1789:			£.	s.	d.
Wheat	66,820	6,983			
Wheat Flour	185,770	3,310			
Rye	37,089	2,718			
Barley	190,197	360			
Malt	125,019	—	76,551	16	1¼ Bo.
Oats	23,997	1,434		Nil. Dr.	
Oatmeal	537	194			
Beans	14,374	4,126			
Pease	8,931	238			
Scotland, 1789:					
Wheat	3,289	—			
Wheat Flour	2,346	—			
Rye	139	—			
Barley	19,127	—			
Barley, hulled	100	—			
Bear or Big	10,972	—	5,999	5	0 Bo.
Bearmeal	61	—			
Malt	9,799	—			
Oats	1,402	—			

Oatmeal	5,118	—	
Pease and beans	222	—	
Groats	12	—	

IMPORTED.

	Quarters.	Duties received.		
		£	s.	d.
England, 1789:				
Wheat	72,379			
Wheat Flour	16,172			
Rye	14,844			
Barley	8,749			
Oats	359,754	4,814	3	7¾
Oatmeal	6,213			
Beans	162			
Pease	99			
Indian corn	54			
Scotland, 1789:				
Wheat	19,722			
Wheat Flour	2,228			
Barley	2,378	1,334	1	9
Oats	63,754			
Pease and beans	130			

The following is an account of the average prices of corn in England and Wales, by the standard Winchester bushel, for the year 1789:

Wheat.		Rye.		Barley.		Oats.		Beans.	
s.	d.	s.	d.	s.	d.	s.	d.	s.	d.
6	4¾	3	8¾	2	10¼	2	0	3	4¾

N.B.—The prices of the finest and coarsest sorts of grain generally exceed and reduce the average price as follows, viz.:

	Wheat.	Rye.	Barley.	Oats.	Beans.
Per bushel	6d.	3d.	3d.	3d.	6d.

THE SPOLIATION OF THE CLERGY IN FRANCE (1790).

Source.—*Reflections on the Revolution in France.* Edmund Burke. Vol. ii. of his Collected Works. LONDON: G. Bell and Sons. 1910.

Burke

Perhaps persons unacquainted with the state of France, on hearing the clergy and the noblesse were privileged in point of taxation, may be led to imagine, that, previous to the Revolution, these bodies had contributed nothing to the state. This is a great mistake. They certainly did not contribute equally with each other, nor either of them equally with the commons. They both, however, contributed largely. Neither nobility nor clergy enjoyed any exemption from the excise on consumable commodities, from duties of custom, or from any of the other numerous *indirect* impositions, which in France, as well as here, make so very large a proportion of all payments to the public. The noblesse paid the capitation. They paid also a land-tax, called the twentieth penny, to the height sometimes of three, sometimes of four, shillings in the pound; both of them *direct* impositions of no light nature, and no trivial produce. The clergy of the provinces annexed by conquest to France, (which in extent make about an eighth part of the whole, but in wealth a much larger proportion,) paid likewise to the capitation and the twentieth penny, at the rate paid by the nobility. The clergy in the old provinces did not pay the capitation; but they had redeemed themselves at the expense of about 24 millions, or a little more than a million sterling. They were exempted from the twentieths: but then they made free gifts; they contracted debts for the state; and they were subject to some other charges, the whole computed at about a thirteenth part of their clear income. They ought to have paid annually about forty thousand pounds more, to put them on a par with the contribution of the nobility.

When the terrors of this tremendous proscription hung over the clergy, they made an offer of a contribution, through the archbishop of Aix, which, for its extravagance, ought not to have been accepted. But it was evidently and obviously more advantageous to the public creditor, than anything which could rationally be promised by the confiscation. Why was it not accepted? The reason is plain—There was no desire that the church should be brought to serve the state. The service of the state was made a pretext to destroy the church. In their way to the destruction of the church they would not scruple to destroy their country: and they have destroyed it. One great end in the project would have been defeated, if the plan of extortion had been adopted in lieu of the scheme of confiscation. The new landed interest connected with the new republic, and connected with it for its very being, could not have been created. This was among the reasons why that extravagant ransom was not accepted.

The madness of the project of confiscation, on the plan that was first pretended, soon became apparent. To bring this unwieldy mass of landed property, enlarged by the confiscation of all the vast landed domain of the crown, at once into market, was obviously to defeat the profits proposed by the confiscation, by depreciating the value of those lands, and indeed of all the landed estates throughout France. Such a sudden diversion of all its circulating money from trade to land, must be an additional mischief. What step was taken? Did the Assembly, on becoming sensible of the inevitable ill effects of their projected sale, revert to the offers of the clergy? No distress could oblige them to travel in a course which was disgraced by any appearance of justice. Giving over all hopes from a general immediate sale, another project seems to have succeeded. They proposed to take stock in exchange for the church lands. In that project great difficulties arose in equalizing the objects to be exchanged. Other obstacles also presented themselves, which threw them back again upon some project of sale. The municipalities had taken an alarm. They would not hear of transferring the whole plunder of the kingdom to the stock-holders in Paris. Many of those municipalities had been (upon system) reduced to the most deplorable indigence. Money was nowhere to be seen. They were therefore led to the point that was so ardently desired. They panted for a currency of any kind which might revive their perishing industry. The municipalities were then to be admitted to a share in the spoil, which evidently rendered the first scheme (if ever it had been seriously entertained) altogether impracticable. Public exigencies pressed upon all sides. The minister of finance reiterated his call for supply with a most urgent, anxious, and boding voice. Thus pressed on all sides, instead of the first plan of converting their bankers into bishops and abbots, instead of paying the old debt, they contracted a new debt, at 3 per cent., creating a new paper currency, founded on an eventual sale of the church lands. They issued this paper currency to satisfy in the first instance chiefly the demands made upon them by the *bank of discount*, the great machine, or paper-mill, of their fictitious wealth.

The spoil of the church was now become the only resource of all their operations in finance, the vital principle of all their politics, the sole security for the existence of their power. It was necessary by all, even the most violent means, to put every individual on the same bottom, and to bind the nation in one guilty interest to uphold this act, and the authority of those by whom it was done. In order to force the most reluctant into a participation of their pillage, they rendered their paper circulation compulsory in all payments. Those who consider the general tendency of their schemes to this one object as a centre, and a centre from which afterwards all their measures radiate, will not think that I dwell too long upon this part of the proceedings of the National Assembly.

To cut off all appearance of connexion between the crown and public justice, and to bring the whole under implicit obedience to the dictators in Paris, the old independent judicature of the parliaments, with all its merits, and all its faults, was wholly abolished. Whilst the parliaments existed, it was evident that the people might some time or other come to resort to them, and rally under the standard of their ancient laws. It became, however, a matter of consideration that the magistrates and officers, in the courts now abolished, *had purchased their places* at a very high rate, for which, as well as for the duty they performed, they received but a very low return of interest. Simple confiscation is a boon only for the clergy;—to the lawyers some appearances of equity are to be observed; and they are to receive compensation to an immense amount. Their compensation becomes part of the national debt, for the liquidation of which there is the one exhaustless fund. The lawyers are to obtain their compensation in the new church paper, which is to march with the new principles of judicature and legislature. The dismissed magistrates are to take their share of martyrdom with the ecclesiastics, or to receive their own property from such a fund, and in such a manner, as all those, who have been seasoned with the ancient principles of jurisprudence, and had been the sworn guardians of property, must look upon with horror. Even the clergy are to receive their miserable allowance out of the depreciated paper, which is stamped with the indelible character of sacrilege, and with the symbols of their own ruin, or they must starve. So violent an outrage upon credit, property, and liberty, as this compulsory paper currency, has seldom been exhibited by the alliance of bankruptcy and tyranny, at any time, or in any nation.

In the course of all these operations, at length comes out the grand *arcanum;*— that in reality, and in a fair sense, the lands of the church (so far as anything certain can be gathered from their proceedings) are not to be sold at all. By the late resolutions of the National Assembly, they are indeed to be delivered to the highest bidder. But it is to be observed, that *a certain portion only of the purchase money is to be laid down.* A period of twelve years is to be given for the payment of the rest. The philosophic purchasers are therefore, on payment of a sort of fine, to be put instantly into possession of the estate. It becomes in some respects a sort of gift to them; to be held on the feudal tenure of zeal to the new establishment. This project is evidently to let in a body of purchasers without money. The consequence will be, that these purchasers, or rather grantees, will pay, not only from the rents as they accrue, which might as well be received by the state, but from the spoil of the materials of buildings, from waste in woods, and from whatever money, by hands habituated to the gripings of usury, they can wring from the miserable peasant. He is to be delivered over to the mercenary and arbitrary discretion of men, who will be stimulated to every species of extortion by the growing demands on the growing profits of an estate held under the precarious settlement of a new political system.

SUSSEX ELECTION PETITIONS (1792).

Source.—*Oldfield's Representative History of Great Britain.* London,
1816.

Oldfield

(A) HORSHAM ELECTION PETITION.

Lord William Gordon and James Baillie, esq., and certain electors in their interest, petitioned in 1790 against the return of Timothy Shelley and Wilson Bradyl, esqrs. The petition was renewed the second session. A committee to try this case met Feb. 16, 1792. The petitions were the same in substance, stating, that the election for Horsham was held June 19, 1790; that Drew Mitchell and John Rawlinson, the baliffs, acted with gross injustice and partiality in favour of the sitting members: that on a poll being demanded, they appointed the Duke of Norfolk's steward, Thomas Charles Medwin, and James Robertson, the steward's clerk, to be the poll-clerks, who rejected legal votes in favour of the petitioners, and received illegal votes for the sitting members, by which means they procured a colourable majority.

The final numbers on the poll were—

T. Shelley, esq.	25
W. Bradyl, esq.	24
Lord W. Gordon	20
J. Baillie, esq.	9

On the 8th of March, 1792, the chairman of the committee reported to the House, that the petitioners were duly elected, and ought to have been returned, and that the sitting members were not duly elected, and ought not to have been returned.

That neither the petitions nor the opposition to them appeared to be frivolous or vexatious. The committee also came to a resolution, which was not reported to the House, that Drew Mitchell and John Rawlinson, the baliffs and returning officers were reprehensible for their conduct. The numbers, according to the votes allowed legal by the committee, were—

Lord W. Gordon	15
J. Baillie, esq.	14

T. Shelley, esq.　　　　10

W. Bradyl, esq.　　　　9

(B) Steyning.

Political Character.

This borough, together with that of Bramber, consists of one street, not more than two-thirds as large as Fetter-lane in London; but constituting *two boroughs*, with a right of sending *four members to Parliament*!!! They formerly elected in conjunction, and intermitted till 31 Henry VI. One part of Bramber is in the centre of the borough of Steyning, and a part of Steyning intersects Bramber in like manner. Inveloped in the dark cloud of legal quibble and intricacy, they present us, like all the rotten boroughs, with a finished picture of political deformity; irregular in their districts, unintelligible in their constitutions, indefinite in their rights, corrupt in the exercise of their functions, contradictory in their respective organizations, and adverse to the ancient established principles of the constitution, and the rights of men.

The right of election has been the subject of litigation in this place for near a century, and has but lately received a final decision from a committee constituted under the authority of 28 Geo. III., to determine the same, upon an appeal from a contrary determination the preceding year.

In 1701, the right was determined to be in the inhabitants paying scot and lot, and not receiving alms.

In 1710, to be in the constables and house-holders (inhabitants) paying scot and lot.

On 16th June, 1715, to be in all such persons as have an estate of inheritance or for life, in burgage-houses or burgage-lands, lying within the said borough.

In 1791, to be in the inhabitants of ancient houses, and houses built on the sites of ancient houses, within the borough of Steyning, being householders, paying scot and lot, and not receiving alms.

In 1792, the select committee appointed to try and determine the merits of the petition of James Martin Lloyd, esq., and others.

Resolved: "That no persons have a right to vote at an election for members to serve in Parliament for the borough of Steyning in respect of any houses within the borough of Bramber, the tithing of Bidlington, or the manors of Charlton or King's Barnes."

The said select committee at the same time also determined,

"That the right of election of members to serve in Parliament for the borough of Steyning, in the county of Sussex, is in the constable and householders, inhabitants within the said borough, paying scot and lot, and not receiving alms."

The houses built on ancient foundations were all the property of the late Sir John Honeywood; the rest belonged to the Duke of Norfolk: and as those of a general description are more numerous, the resolution of 1792, repealing that of 1791, changed the patron, and transferred that influence to the Duke of Norfolk, which the former gave to Sir John Honeywood.

The resolution of 1791 ousted Henry Howard, esq., the present member for Gloster, who had a majority of the householders paying scot and lot, and declared John Curtis, esq., who had only the votes of those persons who inhabited houses built on ancient foundations, duly elected.

The resolution of 1792 established the election of James Martin Lloyd, esq., who polled the identical votes which were deemed illegal the preceding year; and the petitioner *lost* his seat by the same pretensions that Mr. Curtis had obtained one.

These contradictory resolutions have been productive of the same parliamentary inconsistency which distinguished the borough of Saltash, in the Parliament of 1785. Mr. Ambler obtained his seat for that place by the decision of a committee in that year, against the petition of Lord Strathaven, and the same Mr. Curtis, who now succeeded at Steyning, on the right of the corporation to elect the members for Saltash. In 1787, Mr. Lemon, the petitioner, by the determination of a second committee, appointed to try the same question, succeeded on the votes of the burgage-holders, and ousted the Earl of Mornington, sitting member, who had been elected by the corporation.

"Thus two members were sitting in the House of Commons at the same time, and for the same borough, upon the right of different descriptions of electors who had each of them been deemed ineligible in the same Parliament."

This was exactly the case with the representatives of this borough. The inhabitants of houses built on ancient foundations, and the inhabitants in general, have each been declared to possess the right of election; and a member, chosen by each description of voters, has been seated and ousted in the same Parliament.

Since the above decision on the right of election, the Duke of Norfolk has effectually prevented all further contest, by purchasing the whole of Sir John Honeywood's property in Steyning, as he did that of the Marquis of Hertford, at Horsham, and thereby became sole proprietor of both boroughs.

THE RIGHT OF THE FRENCH NATION TO SELF-GOVERNMENT (1792).

Source.—*Cowper's Letters*. Thomas Wright. London: Hodder and Stoughton. 1904. Vol. iv., pp. 332-335.

Cowper's "Letters"

To Lady Hesketh, Dec. 1, 1792.

The French are a vain and childish people, and conduct themselves on this grand occasion with a levity and extravagance nearly akin to madness; but it would have been better for Austria and Prussia to let them alone. All nations have a right to choose their own mode of government, and the sovereignty of the people is a doctrine that evinces itself; for whenever the people choose to be masters they always are so, and none can hinder them. God grant that we may have no revolution here, but unless we have a reform, we certainly shall. Depend upon it, my dear, the hour is come when power founded in patronage and corrupt majorities must govern this land no longer. Concessions too must be made to dissenters of every denomination. They have a right to them, a right to all the privileges of Englishmen, and sooner or later, by fair means or by force, they will have them.

PERORATION IN THE IMPEACHMENT OF WARREN HASTINGS (1794).

Source.—*Speech in the Impeachment of Warren Hastings, Esq.* Edmund Burke. Vol. viii. of his Collected Works. London: G. Bell and Sons. 1908.

Burke

My lords, I have done; the part of the Commons is concluded. With a trembling solicitude we consign this product of our long, long labours to your charge. Take it!—take it! It is a sacred trust. Never before was a cause of such magnitude submitted to any human tribunal.

My lords, at this awful close, in the name of the Commons, and surrounded by them, I attest the retiring, I attest the advancing generations, between which, as a link in the great chain of eternal order, we stand.—We call this nation, we call the world to witness, that the Commons have shrunk from no labour; that we have been guilty of no prevarication; that we have made no compromise with crime; that we have not feared any odium whatsoever, in the long warfare which we have carried on with the crimes—with the vices—with the exorbitant wealth—with the enormous and overpowering influence of Eastern corruption. This war, my lords, we have waged for twenty-two years, and the conflict has been fought at your lordships' bar for the last seven years. My lords, twenty-two years is a great space in the scale of the life of man; it is no inconsiderable space in the history of a great nation. A business which has so long occupied the councils and the tribunals of Great Britain, cannot possibly be huddled over in the course of vulgar, trite, and transitory events. Nothing but some of those great revolutions that break the traditionary chain of human memory, and alter the very face of nature itself, can possibly obscure it. My lords, we are all elevated to a degree of importance by it; the meanest of us will, by means of it, more or less become the concern of posterity, if we are yet to hope for such a thing in the present state of the world as a recording, retrospective, civilized posterity; but this is in the hands of the great Disposer of events; it is not ours to settle how it shall be. My lords, your House yet stands; it stands as a great edifice; but let me say, that it stands in the midst of ruins; in the midst of the ruins that have been made by the greatest moral earthquake that ever convulsed and shattered this globe of ours. My lords, it has pleased Providence to place us in such a state, that we appear every moment to be upon the verge of some great mutations. There is one thing, and one thing only, which defies all mutation; that which existed before the world, and will survive the fabric of the world itself; I mean justice; that justice, which, emanating from the Divinity, has a place in the breast of every one of us, given us for our guide with regard to ourselves, and with regard to others, and which will stand after this globe is burned to ashes, our advocate or our accuser before the great Judge, when He comes to call upon us for the tenor of a well-spent life.

My lords, the Commons will share in every fate with your lordships; there is nothing sinister which can happen to you, in which we shall not be involved; and if it should so happen that we shall be subjected to some of those frightful changes which we have seen — if it should happen that your lordships, stripped of all the decorous distinctions of human society, should, by hands at once base and cruel, be led to those scaffolds and machines of murder, upon which great kings and glorious queens have shed their blood, amidst the prelates, amidst the nobles, amidst the magistrates who supported their thrones, may you in those moments feel that consolation which I am persuaded they felt in the critical moments of their dreadful agony!

My lords, there is a consolation, and a great consolation it is, which often happens to oppressed virtue and fallen dignity; it often happens that the very oppressors and persecutors themselves are forced to bear testimony in its favour. I do not like to go for instances a great way back into antiquity. I know very well that length of time operates so as to give an air of the fabulous to remote events, which lessens the interest and weakens the application of examples. I wish to come nearer to the present time. Your lordships know and have heard, for which of us has not known and heard, of the parliament of Paris? The parliament of Paris had an origin very, very similar to that of the great court before which I stand; the parliament of Paris continued to have a great resemblance to it in its constitution, even to its fall; the parliament of Paris, my lords, WAS; it is gone! It has passed away; it has vanished like a dream! It fell, pierced by the sword of the Compte de Mirabeau. And yet I will say, that that man, at the time of his inflicting the death wound of that parliament, produced at once the shortest and the grandest funeral oration that ever was or could be made upon the departure of a great court of magistracy. Though he had himself smarted under its lash, as every one knows who knows his history (and he was elevated to dreadful notoriety in history), yet when he pronounced the death sentence upon that parliament, and inflicted the mortal wound, he declared that his motives for doing it were merely political, and that their hands were as pure as those of justice itself, which they administered — a great and glorious exit, my lords, of a great and glorious body! And never was a eulogy pronounced upon a body more deserved. They were persons in nobility of rank, in amplitude of fortune, in weight of authority, in depth of learning, inferior to few of those that hear me. My lords, it was but the other day that they submitted their necks to the axe; but their honour was unwounded. Their enemies, the persons who sentenced them to death, were lawyers, full of subtlety; they were enemies, full of malice; yet lawyers full of subtlety, and enemies full of malice, as they were, they did not dare to reproach them with having supported the wealthy, the great, and powerful, and of having oppressed the weak and feeble, in any of their judgments, or of having perverted justice in any one instance whatever, through favour, through interest, or cabal.

My lords, if you must fall, may you so fall! But if you stand, and stand I trust you will, together with the fortune of this ancient monarchy—together with the ancient laws and liberties of this great and illustrious kingdom, may you stand as unimpeached in honour as in power; may you stand not as a substitute for virtue, but as an ornament of virtue, as a security for virtue; may you stand long, and long stand the terror of tyrants; may you stand the refuge of afflicted nations; may you stand a sacred temple, for the perpetual residence of an inviolable justice.

GEORGE III. ASSAULTED BY THE MOB (1795).

Source.—*Letters of Princess Elizabeth of England.* Edited by Philip Yorke. London: Fisher Unwin. 1898.

Letters of Princess Elizabeth

To Lady Harcourt, Wednesday, 5th July, 1795.

I am sure you will be anxious to know how we all are, my dear Ly. H., after yesterday's horrors. It is impossible to paint to you in any degree what we have gone through since we arrived in Town; but I trust in that all-merciful Providence, who has saved our dear King in so wonderful a manner, that the great Crisis is now over.

In going to the House, a bullet was shot through the Kg. coach; which undoubtedly was intended to penetrate elsewhere. This is a most Shocking thought; however, thank God, it went harmlessly through the glass opposite, and shot out a round piece the size of a small bullet. Some of the Servants saw it fall. That not answering their wicked ends, they threw stones several times at him; but he came home well, and perfectly composed. The mob followed the Coach in an insolent manner, moaning and screaming "peace, no War," "give us Bread," "Down with Pitt," "off with your Guards" (which he was attended with to the house, I mean home).

Everybody is well to-day, though much agitated with the thoughts of the Play; but I trust great care will be taken. More you shall hear from me when my mind is easier. God bless you; and believe me,

Yrs. affly.,
E.

THE MUTINY AT THE NORE (1797).

Source.—*Annual Register*. Vol. xxxix., pp. 214 *et seq.* of *History of Europe.*

"Annual Register"

The suppression of the disturbances among the seamen at Portsmouth, without recurring to violent measures, and by granting their petitions, occasioned universal satisfaction, and it was hoped that the causes of their discontent being thus effectually removed, no further complaints would arise to spread alarm throughout the nation. But these reasonable expectations were in a short time wholly disappointed by a fresh mutiny that broke out in the fleet at the Nore, on the twenty-second of May.

The crews on that day took possession of their respective ships, elected delegates to preside over them, and to draw up a statement of their demands, and transmit them to the lords of the admiralty. These demands went much farther than those of the seamen at Portsmouth and Plymouth, and from their exorbitancy did not appear entitled to the same indulgence. On the sixth of June, in the morning, the fleet at the Nore was joined by the *Agamemnon, Leopard, Ardent,* and *Isis* men of war, together with the *Ranger* sloop, which ships had deserted from the fleet under admiral Duncan. When the admiral found himself deserted by part of his fleet, he called his own ship's crew together, and addressed them in the following speech:

"My Lads,

"I once more call you together with a sorrowful heart, from what I have lately seen, the disaffection of the fleets: I call it disaffection, for the crews have no grievances. To be deserted by my fleet, in the face of an enemy, is a disgrace which, I believe, never before happened to a British admiral; nor could I have supposed it possible. My greatest comfort under God is that I have been supported by the officers, seamen, and mariners of this ship: for which, with a heart overflowing with gratitude, I request you to accept my sincere thanks. I flatter myself much good may result from your example, by bringing those deluded people to a sense of their duty, which they owe, not only to their king and country, but to themselves.

"The British navy has ever been the support of that liberty which has been handed down to us by our ancestors, and which I trust we shall maintain to the latest posterity; and that can only be done by unanimity and obedience. The ship's company, and others, who have distinguished themselves by their loyalty and good order, deserve to be, and doubtless will be, the favourites of a grateful country. They will also have, from their inward feelings, a comfort which will be lasting, and not like the floating and false confidence of those who have swerved from their duty.

"It has often been my pride, with you to look into the Texel, and see a foe which dreaded coming out to meet us: my pride is now humbled indeed! my feelings are not easily to be expressed! our cup has overflowed and made us wanton. The all-wise Providence has given us this check, as a warning, and I hope we shall improve by it. On Him then let us trust, where our only security can be found. I find there are many good men among us; for my own part, I have had full confidence of all in this ship; and once more beg to express my approbation of your conduct.

"May God, who has thus far conducted you, continue to do so; and may the British navy, the glory and support of our country, be restored to its wonted splendour, and be not only the bulwark of Britain, but the terror of the world.

"But this can only be effected by a strict adherence to our duty and obedience; and let us pray that the almighty God may keep us in the right way of thinking.

"God bless you all."

At an address so unassuming, modest, and pious, and so well calculated, from its simplicity and truth, to touch the human heart, the whole ship's crew were dissolved in tears. They declared, by every expression they could devise, their resolution to abide by the admiral in life or death. Their example was followed by all the other ships, besides those already mentioned. And the admiral, notwithstanding the defection of so considerable a part of his squadron, repaired to his station, off the coast of Holland, to watch the motions of the Dutch fleet; and resolved, still, not to decline, should it offer him battle.

The principal person at the head of this mutiny was one Richard Parker, a man of good natural parts, and some education, and of a remarkably bold and resolute character. Admiral Buckner, the commanding officer at the Nore, was directed by the lords of the admiralty to inform the seamen, that their demands were totally inconsistent with the good order and regulations necessary to be observed in the navy, and could not for that reason be complied with; but that on returning to their duty, they would receive the king's pardon for their breach of obedience. To this offer Parker replied by a declaration, that the seamen had unanimously determined to keep possession of the fleet, until the lords of the admiralty had repaired to the Nore, and redressed the grievances which had been laid before them.

In order to put an end with all possible expedition to a mutiny that appeared so dangerous, lord Spencer, lord Arden, and admiral Young, hastened immediately to Sheerness, and held a board, at which Parker and the other delegates attended; but their behaviour was so audacious, that the lords of the admiralty returned to town without the least success. The principal article of complaint, on the part of the mutineers, was the unequal distribution of prize-money, for the omission of which they much blamed their fellow seamen at Portsmouth. On the return of the lords of the admiralty from Sheerness, a proclamation was issued, offering his majesty's pardon to all such of the mutineers as should immediately return to their duty: intimating, at the same time, that admiral Buckner was the proper person to be applied to on such an occasion. All the buoys, by order of government, were removed from the mouth of the Thames, and the neighbouring coast; from which precaution, any ships, that should attempt to get away, would be in danger of running a-ground. Great preparations, also, were made, at Sheerness, against an attack from the mutinous ships, which had manifested some strong indications of an intention to bombard that place; and furnaces and hot balls were kept ready.

Emboldened by the strength of men and shipping in their hands, and resolved to persevere in their demands till they had extorted a compliance, the mutineers proceeded to secure a sufficiency of provisions for that purpose, by seizing two vessels laden with stores, and sent notice ashore that they intended to block up the Thames; and cut off all communication between London and the sea, in order to force government to a speedy accession to their terms. They began the execution of this menace by mooring four of their vessels across the mouth of the river, and stopping several ships that were coming from the metropolis.

They now altered the system of their delegation, and to prevent too much power from being lodged in the hands of any man, the office of president was entrusted to no one longer than a day. This they did to secure themselves from the attempts to betray them, which might result from the offers held out to those in whom they were obliged to place confidence and authority, were those to possess such a trust for any time. They also compelled those ships, the crews of which they suspected of wavering in the cause, to take their station in the midst of the others. But, notwithstanding these precautions, two vessels eluded their vigilance, and made their escape.

These transactions, while they excited the greatest alarm in the nation, were violently reprobated by the seamen belonging to the two divisions of the fleet lying at Portsmouth and at Plymouth. Each of them addressed an admonition to their fellow-seamen at the Nore, warmly condemning their proceedings as a scandal to the name of British seamen, and exhorting them to be content with the indulgence already granted by government, and to return to their duty without insisting on more concessions than had been demanded by the rest of the navy.

But these warnings proved ineffectual. The reinforcement of the four ships lately arrived, and the expectation of being joined by others, induced them to per-sist in their demands. The committee of delegates, on board the *Sandwich*, came to a determination to commission lord Northesk, whom they had kept in confine-ment in the *Montague*, of which he was the commander, to repair to the king in the name of the fleet, and to acquaint him with the conditions on which they were willing to deliver up the ships. The petition, which he was charged to lay before the king, was highly respectful and loyal to him, but very severe on his ministers, and they required an entire compliance with every one of their demands, threat-ening, on the refusal of any, to put immediately to sea. Lord Northesk readily undertook to be the bearer of their petition, but told them, that, from the unrea-sonableness of their demands, he could not flatter them with the hope of success. Confiding in him, they said, as the seamen's friend, they had entrusted him with this mission, on pledging his honour to return, with a clear and positive answer, within fifty-four hours.

Lord Northesk departed accordingly for London, and was introduced, by lord Spencer, to the king. But no answer being returned to the message, and information being brought to the fleet, that the nation at large highly disapproved of their proceedings, great divisions took place among the delegates, and several of the ships deserted the others, not, however, without much contest and bloodshed. The mutineers, despairing, now, of accomplishing their designs, struck the red flag, which they had hoisted as the signal of mutiny, and restored a free passage to the trade of the metropolis. Every ship was now left at its own command, and they all gradually returned to obedience, though, on board of some, violent struggles happened between the mutineers and the loyal parties.

The principal conductor of the mutiny, Richard Parker, was seized and imprisoned, and after a solemn trial, that lasted three days, on board of the *Neptune*, he was sentenced to death. He suffered with great coolness and intrepidity, acknowledging the justice of his sentence, and expressing his hope, that mercy might be extended to his associates. But it was judged necessary to make public examples of the principal and most guilty, who were accordingly tried, and, after full proof of their criminality, condemned and executed. Others were ordered to be whipped; but a considerable number remained under sentence of death till after the great victory obtained, over the Dutch fleet, by admiral Duncan: when his majesty sent a general pardon to those unhappy men; who were, at that period, confined on board a prison ship in the river Thames.

ENGLAND AND THE DIRECTORY (1797).

Source.—*Correspondence of the First Earl of Malmesbury*, London, 1844. Vol. iii., pp. 577 *et seq.*

Correspondence of Malmesbury

Letter from Lord Malmesbury to Mr. Pitt, Calais. Sept. 18th. 1797.

My dear Sir,—

Although I shall in a very few hours have the pleasure of seeing you, I cannot delay till then thanking you most sincerely for your two last very comfortable private letters. No consolation could ever come at a moment when it is more wanted. I almost feel guilty of ingratitude in making so ill a return to it, as that of leaving Lisle so rapidly, notwithstanding, God knows, my will by no means consented to this act. I trust this will appear in everything I have said and done, and that nothing has been omitted on my part to obtain what I know to be *your first wish*, and which I can safely say was also *mine*. The having failed in it hurts me still the more, as we infallibly should have succeeded had not the *political earthquake* of the 4th of September taken place. But success being impossible, the next best comfort is, the having failed without discredit to myself; and if, when I have the pleasure to meet you, I should be assured of it, I shall feel comfort fully equal to that in which I began this letter, by thanking you.

I am, &c.

(Signed) Malmesbury.

Letter from Lord Malmesbury to Mr. Canning, Calais, Monday, 9 p.m., Sept. 18th, 1797.

My dear Canning,—

If the date of the place from whence this letter is written surprises you, let me refer you to my public despatch for all the wholesale reasons, and desire you to wait for the more detailed one till to-morrow evening, or probably Wednesday morning, when I hope we shall meet. Your private letter to me by Herslet, although on an uncomfortable subject, afforded me very great consolation; since I not only perceive you are prepared for my return, but prepared for it in a way which totally disperses the few apprehensions I had, lest my conduct, under the present circumstances, might not in every respect have met every approbation.

From what you say, I am now certain it will; and it gives me the more pleasure, from a consciousness that I never in my life acted more rightly.

I am too fatigued to go on to-night with the messengers, but we sail to-morrow at nine a.m.; and on the whole, I had rather you should read my story than hear it told by me. I have much to say to you, and to some others, but I should not like to hold forth before a Cabinet.

I am infinitely obliged to you (in the strict sense of the word) for your very friendly and attentive goodness in endeavouring to replace all that I lost by the cruel accident which has happened to poor Brooks. Your principal does not partake of this sort of feeling; and he has as few of this species of human *imperfections* as any being called *human* can pretend to.

Let us hear from you on our arrival. I shall drive at once to my own house, and if possible, before twelve o'clock on Wednesday.

I am, &c.
(Signed) MALMESBURY.

Extract of a Despatch from Lord Malmesbury to Lord Grenville, Calais, 19th Sept., 1797.

There can be little doubt, from the language and manner of the French Plenipotentiaries, that there is a fixed determination on the part of the French Government to continue war with England; and that if in any part of their behaviour or conversation with me there appeared a contrary intention, it was solely with a view to avoid, if possible, that the odium of breaking off the Negotiation should be imputed entirely to them. They, however, have managed this with so very little ability—what they have done has been so positive, and what they have said so vague—that it is difficult even for the most prejudiced minds to entertain a doubt on this subject.

The whole of my official Correspondence since the event of the 4th of September will, I trust, have so far prepared your Lordship for what has now happened, that, although it may very justly cause concern, it will not create surprise. Disposed as I was to pay attention to whatever I heard from the late members of the French Legation, as well from their knowledge of their own country, as from my having, on every important point, always found their information correct, I could never allow my opinion to go with them on this particular point; and although the satisfaction of having judged rightly cannot, on an occasion like this, be very great, yet the not having misled your Lordship diminishes, to a certain degree, the regret I feel on having failed in the great end of my Mission.

It would be vain to search for any rational motive for such a conduct as the Directory have thought proper to adopt, or to endeavour to explain on what grounds they can prefer a hazardous and unpromising continuation of a war, become extremely unpopular, to an advantageous and honourable peace, and one which, I am confident, would have had the approbation of the whole French nation. The solution of this difficulty cannot be found either in the internal situation of France, or in its present relative position to other powers, but must be sought for in the daring and inconsiderate character of the two governing members of the Directory, Barras and Rewbell. The success which has attended their late very bold undertaking appears to have given them the most implicit confidence in their own abilities, and in the strength of their party; and they never at any time appeared to have any fixed system, or to look forward beyond the circumstances of the moment.

THE BATTLE OF THE NILE (OR ABOUKIR BAY) (1798).

Source.—*Annual Register.* Vol. xl., pp. 142 *et seq.* of *History of Europe.*

"Annual Register"

It was the first of August before the Pharos of Alexandria was got sight of by the squadron, who were then steering direct for it towards the S.S.E. and as they approached discovered a wood of masts in the harbour. The advanced ships (the *Alexander* and *Leander* about two leagues a head) made signal for having discovered ships of war to eastward. The admiral, who, with the bulk of the squadron, was in close order of sailing, being thus directed to a view of the long sought-for fight, immediately altered his course accordingly, and made signal to recal those on the look-out. The *Culloden* was then about two leagues to the eastward of the admiral, and, after some time and signals exchanged, obtained leave to cast off the vessel towed from off Coron. The *Alexander* and *Leander*, who had run in nearer Alexandria, were thereby obliged to hawl more to the wind than between N.N.W. and N.W. in order to round the point off Aboukir; which threw them considerably later than the main body; who sailing with a free wind reached about, or soon after five o'clock, the point; which having rounded and got the bay fairly open, the admiral hawled up on the lar-board tack, under an easy sail, probably for the purpose of viewing the situation of the enemy, or more likely for giving time for those of his own squadron to close; the *Culloden* being still about two leagues distant in the N.W. quarter. While the *Alexander* and *Leander* were still farther distant in the W.S.W. the squadron of the enemy, which shewed 13 sail of the line of battle, were but a few miles off, bearing from S.W. to south, and anchored in a line extending nearly N.W. and S.E. with their admiral's flag on board a three deck ship in the centre, and four frigates, with several gun-vessels, dispersed inside towards the van and rear.

The squadron did not remain long with their heads from the enemy. The admiral speedily determined on what plan of attack was to be adopted. He gave orders, by signal, to prepare to anchor by the stern, and wore with the whole squadron together by signal. That manœuvre at once changed the situation of the squadron, by giving the lead to those, who were, while their heads were to the offing, dropping a-stern to join their situation in the rear, in the order of sailing: or, as some have alleged, loitered a-stern from an unwillingness to be drawn off even a few hundred yards from the enemy. If such were the sentiments of any, they were now indulged by the admiral bearing up toward the van of the enemy, and making the signal to form the line of battle a-head, or most convenient: that is, for each ship to fall in as their situation at the time best suited, without regard to the established order of battle.

On that occasion, there were such displays of emulation by each ship to gain an advanced post in the attack, as must have tended to inspire each other with an invincible confidence. But so alert were the whole, that no one ship could gain the point of getting a-head of another, who had the advantage of laying their heads towards the enemy. The admiral, as they were drawing into a form of battle, made the signal to attack the enemy's van and centre: and soon after, added the signal for a close engagement, which was kept flying.

The wind, which was between N.W. and N.N.W., had been a fresh top gallant sail breeze, and, though moderated as the day drew towards a close, still swelled out the lighter sails. Before the *Goliah* (the leading ship) had approached within a mile of the enemy's van ships, they commenced a brisk cannonade with their starboard guns, as did the batteries at the castle of Becquires and the gun-vessels, which galled the British squadron much as they closed. But the situation of the enemy's anchorage, and the shallowness of the water around, rendered it impossible to evade that annoyance. It was therefore borne with a firmness worthy of their character. The period was but short when it became theirs to return the annoyance. The gallant leader[10] in the *Goliah*, on that occasion displayed a conduct which shewed him worthy of the post he had taken. Keeping his ship under all convenient working sail, he kept as near to the edge of the bank as the depth of water would permit, and passing a-head of the enemy's van ship, *Le Guerrier*, poured into her a most destructive fire; and bearing round up shortened sail,[11] and anchored by the stern inside of the second of the enemy's line, *Le Conquerant*.

The *Zealous* followed in the track of the *Goliah*, but not so far, having dropped her stern anchor, so as to preserve a situation on the inside bow of *Le Guerrier*, whom she handled in the severest manner without being exposed to annoyance in return. The *Orion* next followed, and passing to windward of the *Zealous*, and round her, plying her larboard guns on *Le Guerrier*, while they bore, continued on a S.E. course, and passed the inside of the *Goliah*: when, being annoyed by a frigate's fire, she yawed as much as was necessary to bring her starboard guns to bear, and gave her so complete a dose as to silence her for ever. Then hawling round towards the enemy's line, she dropped the starboard bower anchor inside between the third and fourth ships from their van, and with some exertions, by spreading

[10] The passing around the bow of the enemy's van and inside of their line appears to have originated with the leader, Captain Foley, as no signal was made to direct such a manœuvre, and the suggestion, so apropos, was highly worthy of a seaman having ready and clear ideas of what appertained to his profession. The example was followed by four others of those who composed the van, and the advantage which was derived from that manœuvre may be best calculated by a reference to the result. This kind of initiative may well have been learnt from Nelson's notable manœuvre in the Battle of St. Vincent in 1797.

[11] The wind had become so moderate that it was not necessary to furl the sails, that the anchor might hold; they were only hauled as close up as was possible, which circumstance allowed the men to remain at their quarters on the principal batteries.

all her after-sail, (probably to force her keel over the ground, which it most likely touched) got her swung round abreast of *L'Aquilon*, who had, without annoyance, suffered the *Orion* to place herself in this situation. The *Theseus*, who followed the *Orion*, passed between the *Zealous* and *Le Guerrier*, so close to the latter, (whose foremast was by this time over the side) only preserving sufficient distance to avoid entangling her rigging with the jib-boom of the enemy's ship, and when abreast of her bow, poured in a broadside, until then reserved, the effect of which on the enemy was instantaneous. The main and mizen-masts were also brought down. Thus, in less than fifteen minutes was the van ship of this line reduced to a mere hulk, incumbered with the wreck of her own masts and yards, and doubtless the crew much mutilated. That destructive broadside was given just as the sun dipped in the horizon; after which the *Theseus* passed on the outside of the *Goliah*, and dropped her stern-anchor a-head of her; and thus was placed inside of the third ship of the enemy, *La Spartiate*, and had commenced the cannonade about the time or before her leader, the *Orion*, was got completely placed, from the little interruptions before-mentioned.

The *Audacious* followed next, and passing between *Le Guerrier* and *Conquerant*, increased the misfortunes of those ill-fated ships, by a destructive fire, and afterwards dropped her stern-anchor, so as to preserve her station inside bow of the latter, over whom the *Goliah* had already got a decided superiority, by the comparative fire maintained. The breeze by this time (as above observed) had lessened as the day closed: most probably too it had been lulled the more by the effect of the cannonade, which had for some time been maintained: hence the ships which were in the rear of the British squadron were not enabled to close with the celerity suitable to their ardour on that occasion.

The *Vanguard* was the follower of the *Audacious*; but did not, like the five who had preceded her, pass the enemy's line: the rank of the admiral (whose flag this ship bore) gave him a privilege of deviating from the example of his leaders, whose manœuvres were to be guided by his direction: she was anchored by the stern on the outside, and close to the third ship from the van, *Le Spartiate*. Her followers respectively passed on a-head of their leader, anchoring by the stern as they came up on the outside as the admiral had done. Thus the *Minotaur*, *Defence*, and *Swift-sure*, took position a-breast of the fourth, fifth, and sixth ships from the van; by which arrangement it was left for the *Bellerophon* to attack the French admiral's ship, *L'Orient*, of three decks:[12] nor was the undertaking shrunk from, because of the apparent inequality of the contest: the *Bellerophon's* stern-anchor was dropped on the outside bow of *L'Orient*, whose collection of heavy batteries was reserved for the closing. The effect of these will be best judged of by the reference to the list of killed and wounded of the hardy assailants, in which stands enrolled the names of almost every officer of that ship. By that time the day was so much closed, as to obscure from general view the conduct of each ship; particularly towards the centre, which was covered with the clouds of smoke blown thither from the van,

[12] The difference of force between *L'Orient* and *Bellerophon*, or any other of the squadron, by estimating the weight of ball fired from one broadside of each, was above seven to three, and the weight of ball from *L'Orient's* lower deck alone exceeded that from the whole broadside of the *Bellerophon*.

by the light breeze which yet continued. Under these circumstances, the *Majestic*, who followed the *Bellerophon*, had to grope for an antagonist; in doing which, it is said, she found her jib-boom had entered the main rigging of one of the enemy's ships a-stern of their admiral; by whom, she was most severely treated while thus entangled: but, after some time, she swung clear, and avenged herself completely on another of the enemy farther astern.

Having thus got all the ships into action, that had formed the body of the squadron, the *Culloden*, who had been detained by the towing of the wine-vessel, may now be looked after; also the *Alexander* and *Leander*, who had been thrown out a-stern, by their having been on the look-out towards Alexandria.

It was with extreme mortification observed, before the day had closed, that the former had run a-ground on a shoal, which was found to extend N.E. from the point on which the castle stood. It may be better imagined than described what were the feelings of the gallant commander and crew of that ship, to be so arrested in their passage to the participation of the fatigues and glory of the combat then depending. The loss of the assistance of such a ship, on so important occasion too, must have excited emotions of deep regret among those engaged, many of whom had witnessed, on an important and splendid occasion in the preceding year, how eminently that ship, under the command of the same officer, and with the same crew, had been distinguished.—Great as the loss of this ship's assistance was, it yielded some consolation to conclude, that her running a-ground served as a beacon to induce the two ships (*Alexander* and *Leander*, then to the westward of her) to hawl more out to the offing than they might otherwise have done, from an anxiety to be as soon as possible up to the assistance of their companions; in which case the assistance of two ships would have been lost instead of the *Culloden*. The *Mutine* brig made towards her, and remained to render her assistance in getting off the ground; and the *Leander*, in passing, had communication to know if she could render her effectual aid: that being judged impracticable, she followed her companion, the *Alexander*, who, having rounded the end of the shoal, was then steering for the centre of the enemy, under all sail: nor did she shorten any, until closed with the French admiral's ship, whom she passed and anchored in a most judicious position inside of that tremendous ship, whom she attacked with a brisk-ness, and maintained with such vivacity, as indicated the impatience of the crew in having been thrown out so long from entering into the action.

Without pretending to minute accuracy with regard to time, this may be stated to have taken place about, or soon after eight o'clock. Soon after, the *Leander* ran in under the stern of the fifth ship; and, anchoring there, took a position whereby she could, without annoyance, fire her guns of one side in the stern of *Le Peuple Souverain*, and those of the other side into the bows of *La Franklin*. It is unnecessary to remark on what must have been the effect of so destructive a raking fire, even from a ship of the *Leander's* small force.

Thus did each of the British ships enter into action. The result shews the man-ner in which each performed its duty. By the time the last-mentioned ships got placed in their respective positions, those which formed the van of the enemy were silenced, and some had struck. Their submission had extended as far as the fourth ship, about nine o'clock. And, soon after, *L'Orient*, in their centre, was discovered to be on fire, which spread with such rapidity that she was soon in a general blaze, and precluded even a shadow of hope for her preservation. The cannonade was, in the meantime, maintained with equal briskness by the British ships, whose opponents had not yet surrendered, while some of them, very much sickened, were barely able to maintain resistance.

While the flames were consuming *L'Orient*, great were the exertions made by the *Alexander* to remove to such distance as her captain judged necessary to save her from danger of being covered with the wreck of her unfortunate antagonist. About ten o'clock, the fire had reached *L'Orient's* magazine, when she blew up with a most tremendous explosion, by which fragments of her wreck were thrown to a considerable distance on every side; and those ships who were nearest to the place of the explosion, were for some time completely obscured, by the thick column of smoke which spread around. The cannonade at that moment ceased, and a silence ensued, strongly expressive of the awe with which the minds of the combatants were impressed by that dreadful event.

That impression appeared to be effaced, by the recollection that there was still duty left to be performed; for, in about ten minutes after, the cannonade was renewed around the spot where *L'Orient* had exploded, and in a few minutes was maintained with vivacity, and continued with little abatement until after midnight, when it became slacker, with some intermissions, indicating the exhausted state of the combatants, by the fatigue already undergone;[13] but the firing did not entirely cease until three o'clock.

Thursday morning, the second of August. —When the day opened, how different was the prospect from that which the preceding evening had closed! The greatest part of the ships, which formed the van of the French line, dismasted, and all struck! Not a vestige of their admiral's ship to be seen! The frigate (*La Sêrieuse*), whom the *Orion* had silenced the preceding evening, now sunk! The *Bellerophon* was observed several miles to the eastward along shore, at anchor, dismasted. Some of the British ships, which had attacked and defeated the van, now shifted more towards the rear, and others moving thither, to complete the conquest of the enemy's ships. In that part, this led to a recommencement of the cannonade, in the outset of which, a frigate (*L'Artémise*), in the centre, displayed a conduct mean and unworthy of the squadron to which it was attached. After firing a broad-side, she struck; but, before she was sent to, by any of the British ships, was observed to be on fire, and the crew making for the shore in their boats, where they were so ill received by the natives, that a remnant of them were fain to return, and trust to the generosity of their enemy, whom they had so recently offended by a flagrant breach of the laws of war.

[13] As an instance of the fatigue, it may here be noted, that one of the ships, which were inside of the van, and had finished her duty there, did in the morning, some hours before daylight, weigh her stern anchor for the purpose of going towards the rear, to attack the enemy there; and, as the men unshipped the capstan-bars, many of them lay down among them, being so much overcome with fatigue as to fall asleep, notwithstanding that they must have known the anchor was got up, and the ship then moving toward the enemy, to begin a fresh cannonade.

Without entering into any further detail of the whole, after the cannonade had been long maintained, with some intermissions, it was closed with the surrender of *L'Heureux* and *Mercure*, and dismasting of *Le Tonnant*. The two rear ships, *Le Guillaume Tell* and *Genereux*, observing all their companions either surrendered, or in a disabled state, prepared to get under sail, which they did, without interruption, before two o'clock, and were accompanied by *La Dianne* and *Justice* frigates, neither of whom had been annoyed. *Le Timoleon* made an attempt to follow, but, casting with her head into the bay, and not being alertly managed (probably, not in a manageable state), her head was not got out to the offing, but ran ashore at a little distance from whence she had laid, in the south-east part of the bay, where they set her on fire. The *Zealous*, who was under sail when the rear ships of the enemy left the bay, stood after them; but, as there was not any other then under sail, to accompany and support her, she was called in by the admiral.

There yet remained to be taken possession of, *Le Tonnant*, entirely dismasted, but who had not struck, and had shifted a considerable distance to leeward from her original position. In that state, incapable of moving or helping herself, a message was sent, to demand her surrender, which the captain refused, without the condition of vessels being furnished to carry him and his crew (which he stated to be then 1,500) to France. This requisition was communicated to admiral Nelson, who desired him to be informed, that the surrender must be unconditional, else force would be employed, against which resistance would not avail. These communications were not exchanged till late in the evening of the second, owing to the distance.

Friday morning, the third of August, the French flag was observed to be still displayed on the stump of *Le Tonnant's* main-mast. The admiral made signals to the *Theseus* and *Leander* to attack her. It appeared they had, in some measure, recovered from their late fatigues, by the alertness of their movements. They were soon under the necessary sail; and, on the *Theseus* approaching her rear, the flag of truce was hoisted. An officer was then sent from the *Theseus* to desire the colours to be struck unconditionally, which was complied with. Thus was the close put to that distinguished battle.

Whether a retrospect is had to the unremitting perseverance in continuing the search after the enemy, to the promptness of decision in attacking them when found, or to the skill and intrepidity with which the attack was executed, it is difficult to decide which has the highest claim to admiration. The renown of this action has reached to every part of the globe, and been re-echoed back with the high praises so justly merited.

SUPPLIES GRANTED BY PARLIAMENT FOR NAVY AND ARMY (1800).

Source.—*Annual Register*. Vol. xlii., pp. 160 *et seq.* of *Appendix to Chronicle.*

"Annual Register"

NAVY.

	£	s.	d.
October 1, 1799.			
That 120,000 seamen be employed for two lunar months commencing 1st January, 1800, including 22,696 marines:			
For wages for ditto	444,000	0	0
For victuals for ditto	456,000	0	0
For wear and tear of ships in which they are to serve	720,000	0	0
For ordnance sea service on board such ships	60,000	0	0
October 3.			
For the ordinary establishment of the navy, for two lunar months, commencing 1st January, 1800	121,510	0	0
For the extraordinary establishment of ditto	115,625	0	0
February 10, 1800.			
That 110,000 seamen be employed for eleven lunar months, commencing 26th February, 1800, including 22,696 marines:			
For wages for ditto	2,238,500	0	0
For victuals for ditto	2,229,000	0	0
For wear and tear of ships in which they are to serve	3,630,000	0	0
For ordnance sea service on board such ships	302,500	0	0
February 13.			

	£	s.	d.
For the ordinary of the navy, including half pay to sea and marine officers, for eleven lunar months, commencing 26th February, 1800	685,429	13	11
For buildings and repairs of ships, and other extra works	656,515	0	0
For the probable expense of transport service, for one year, commencing 1st January, 1800	1,300,000	0	0
For the maintenance of prisoners of war in health	500,000	0	0
For the care and maintenance of sick prisoners of war	90,000	0	0
	£13,619,079	13	11

ARMY.

October 3, 1799.			
	£	s.	d.
That 90,047 men be employed for land service, including 5,766 invalids, from 25th December, 1799, to 24th February, 1800:			
For guards, garrisons, and other land-forces in Great Britain, Jersey, Guernsey, and Alderney, and in Holland	510,596	0	0
For forces in the plantations, including Gibraltar, Minorca, the Cape of Good Hope, and New South Wales	166,480	0	0
For the increased rates of subsistence to be paid to innkeepers and others, on quartering soldiers	40,000	0	0
For expenses expected to be incurred in the barrack-master general's department	120,000	0	0
February 13, 1800.			
That 80,275 men be employed for land-service, including 5,792 invalids, from 25th February, 1800:			
For guards, garrisons, and other land-forces in Great Britain, Jersey, Guernsey, and Alderney	2,337,159	8	8
For forces in the plantations, including Gibraltar, Portugal, Minorca, and other stations in the Mediterranean, the Cape of Good Hope, and New South Wales	1,004,480	13	6
For difference between the British and Irish pay of six regiments of foot for service abroad	42,901	19	0

For four troops of dragoons, and sixteen companies of foot stationed in Great Britain for recruiting regiments serving in East India	24,558	3	8
For recruiting and contingencies for land-forces, and extra feed for the cavalry	530,000	0	0
For general and staff-officers, and officers of hospitals	105,054	7	11
For full pay to supernumerary officers	26,230	14	6
For allowance to the paymaster-general of the forces, commissary-general of the musters, &c. &c.	105,747	2	6
For the increased rates of subsistence to be paid to inn-keepers and others, on quartering soldiers	140,000	0	0
For allowance to the non-commissioned officers and private men of the land forces, in lieu of small beer	120,000	0	0
For reduced officers of land-forces and marines	138,979	7	1
For allowances to reduced horse-guards	20	12	11
On account of officers late in the service of the states-general	1,000	0	0
Ditto, of reduced officers of British-American forces	52,500	0	0
For allowances to several reduced officers of ditto	7,500	0	0
For the in and out-pensioners of Chelsea hospital, and the expenses of the hospital	143,310	7	3
For pensions to widows of officers of land forces	20,231	12	0
For expenses incurred, and expected to be incurred in the barrack-master general's department	359,334	0	0
For foreign corps in the service of Great Britain	471,128	12	3
February 24.			
To defray the extraordinary services of the army for 1800	2,500,000	0	0
May 27.			
For the troops of the elector of Bavaria, in the pay of Great Britain, pursuant to treaty	566,688	10	0
July 16.			
For the expense of a royal military asylum for the reception of the children of soldiers	25,000	0	0
	£9,558,951	12	3

HIS MAJESTY'S SPEECH TO THE FIRST UNION PARLIAMENT (1801).

Source.—*Annual Register.* Vol. xliii., pp. 207 *et seq.* of *State Papers.*

"Annual Register"

His Majesty's Speech to both Houses, on opening the Imperial Parliament, 2d February, 1801.

My Lords and Gentlemen,

At a crisis so important to the interests of my people, I derive great satisfaction from being enabled, for the first time, to avail myself of the advice and assistance of the parliament of my united kingdom of Great Britain and Ireland.

This memorable era, distinguished by the accomplishment of a measure calculated to augment and consolidate the strength and resources of the empire, and to cement more closely the interests and affections of my subjects, will, I trust, be equally marked by that vigour, energy, and firmness, which the circumstances of our present situation peculiarly require.

The unfortunate course of events on the continent, and the consequences which must be expected to result from it, cannot fail to be matter of anxiety and concern, to all who have a just feeling for the security and independence of Europe.

Your astonishment, as well as your regret, must be excited by the conduct of those powers, whose attention, at such a period, appears to be more engaged in endeavours to weaken the naval force of the British empire, which has hitherto opposed so powerful an obstacle to the inordinate ambition of France, than in concerting the means of mutual defence against their common and increasing danger.

The representations which I directed to be made to the court of Petersburgh, in consequence of the outrages committed against the ships, property, and persons of my subjects, have been treated with the utmost disrespect: and the proceedings of which I complained have been aggravated by subsequent acts of injustice and violence. Under these circumstances, a convention has been concluded by that court, with those of Copenhagen and Stockholm; the object of which, as avowed by one of the contracting parties, is to renew their former engagements for establishing by force a new code of maritime law, inconsistent with the rights, and hostile to the interests of this country.

In this situation I could not hesitate as to the conduct which it became me to pursue.

I have taken the earliest measures to repel the aggressions of this hostile confederacy, and to support those principles which are essential to the maintenance of our naval strength, and which are grounded on the system of public law so long established and recognised in Europe. I have, at the same time, given such assurances as manifest my disposition to renew my ancient relations with those powers, whenever it can be done consistently with the honour of my crown, and with a just regard to the safety of my subjects.

You will, I am persuaded, omit nothing on your part that can afford me the most vigorous and effectual support, in my firm determination to maintain, to the utmost, against every attack, the naval rights and the interests of my empire.

GENTLEMEN OF THE HOUSE OF COMMONS,

I have directed the estimates for the several branches of the public service to be laid before you. Deeply as I lament the continued necessity of adding to the burdens of my people, I am persuaded you will feel with me the importance of providing effectual means for those exertions which are indispensably requisite for the honour and security of the country.

MY LORDS AND GENTLEMEN,

I am confident that your deliberations will be uniformly directed to the great object of improving the benefits of that happy union, which, by the blessing of Providence, has now been effected; and of promoting to the utmost the prosperity of every part of my dominions.

Lector House believes that a society develops through a two-fold approach of continuous learning and adaptation, which is derived from the study of classic literary works spread across the historic timeline of literature records. Therefore, we aim at reviving, repairing and redeveloping all those inaccessible or damaged but historically as well as culturally important literature across subjects so that the future generations may have an opportunity to study and learn from past works to embark upon a journey of creating a better future.

This book is a result of an effort made by Lector House towards making a contribution to the preservation and repair of original ancient works which might hold historical significance to the approach of continuous learning across subjects.

HAPPY READING & LEARNING!

LECTOR HOUSE LLP
E-MAIL: lectorpublishing@gmail.com